"Though many Reformed Christians talk about TULIP, too often they neglect the rich soil from which that flower springs: the Canons of Dort. Yet this historic statement of faith abounds with biblical truth wisely designed to encourage love for the triune God and evangelism of the lost. DeYoung's brief exposition of the canons is ideal for personal study, doctrine classes, and small groups that aim to better understand the controversy over Arminianism and why the Reformed doctrine of salvation by grace alone leads us to live for the glory of God alone."

Joel R. Beeke, President and Professor of Systematic Theology and Homiletics, Puritan Reformed Theological Seminary; Pastor, Heritage Reformed Congregation, Grand Rapids, Michigan; author, *Reformed Preaching*

"Why would a finger-on-the-pulse, contemporary pastor-theologian like Kevin DeYoung take us on a journey four hundred years into the past to a place few of us could locate on a map to meet people whose names we are unable to pronounce? And why should we join him? I can think of at least three reasons. As twenty-first-century Christians we need to (1) remember that 'those who cannot remember the past are condemned to repeat it'; (2) meet believers who thought deeply and cared passionately about the glory of God in the gospel; and (3) put roots into nourishing theological soil that will give clarity to our thinking, create stability in our living, and put doxology into our serving. *Grace Defined and Defended* helps us to do all three."

Sinclair B. Ferguson, Chancellor's Professor of Systematic Theology, Reformed Theological Seminary; Teaching Fellow, Ligonier Ministries

"DeYoung manages to bring an event from four hundred years ago right back into the present needs of the church and of theology, with clear style, solid theological insights, pastoral tone, and helpful clarification of difficult but biblical notions. This is a book that helps us understand that Dort certainly is not just history and we must keep working with its message."

Herman Selderhuis, Professor of Church History, Theological University Apeldoorn; Director, Refo500

"I am so encouraged to see a book on the Canons of Dort—not only because it explores the finely tuned confession of Reformed thinking but also because it highlights the precision of biblical fidelity. DeYoung's concise summary of this catechism's emphasis on the doctrines of grace is so vitally needed in our late-modern culture, which tends to prioritize emotional reasoning over thoughtful reflection. This book is a clarion call for all Christians to avoid cognitive distortions and to root their lives in a historic, confessional faith that is both biblically and theologically faithful to the Scriptures."

Stephen T. Um, Senior Minister, Citylife Presbyterian Church of Boston; author, *Micah For You*

GRACE
DEFINED AND
DEFENDED

Other Crossway Books by Kevin DeYoung

Crazy Busy: A (Mercifully) Short Book about a (Really) Big Problem (2013)

Don't Call It a Comeback (2011)

The Hole in Our Holiness: Filling the Gap between Gospel Passion and the Pursuit of Godliness (2012)

Taking God at His Word: Why the Bible Is Knowable, Necessary, and Enough, and What That Means for You and Me (2014)

The Ten Commandments: What They Mean, Why They Matter, and Why We Should Obey Them (2018)

What Does the Bible Really Teach about Homosexuality? (2015)

What Is the Mission of the Church?: Making Sense of Social Justice, Shalom, and the Great Commission (coauthor, 2011)

Children's Books

The Biggest Story: How the Snake Crusher Brings Us Back to the Garden (2015)

The Biggest Story ABC (2017)

GRACE DEFINED AND DEFENDED

*What a 400-Year-Old Confession Teaches Us about
Sin, Salvation, and the Sovereignty of God*

Kevin DeYoung

WHEATON, ILLINOIS

LB		29	28	27	26	25	24	23	22	21	20	19
15	14	13	12	11	10	9	8	7	6	5	4	3	2	1

To my home church,
Hager Park Reformed Church (Jenison, MI),
where I first learned TULIP and the doctrines of grace

Contents

Introduction

In Praise of Precision

The first car I owned was a 1995 Dodge Neon, and it was a lemon. Besides being a girly car (as my eventual wife told me when I picked her up for one of our first dates), the cute little white powder puff (the car, not my wife!) never worked properly. It had alignment problems and electrical problems and transmission problems, of the problems I can remember.

The worst problem was that it would sometimes, for no discernible reason, just stop. Like at a traffic light, or turning a corner, or when sneezed upon by hummingbirds. The car would shut down completely. The dashboard would go dark and the vehicle would slow to a halt.

Being an auto repair genius, I learned that the only thing to do in this situation was to pop the hood (if I could find that lever), walk around to the front, locate a silver-looking thingy, and bang on it five or six times with a ratchet. Sure enough, the car revved up again. Once married, I was able to pass along this valuable expertise to Trisha. She too would know the joys of hammering away at a deceased car while motioning a line of cars to pass by our Neon roadkill.

It wasn't long before my wife found this method of "dealing with the problem" to be less than satisfactory. Calling into question my mechanical acumen, she had the gall to suggest that a trip to a certified auto mechanic was in order. The mechanic was able to ascertain that the silver thingy we kept banging was actually the alternator, the invaluable piece of machinery that supplies power to the electrical system while the engine is running. It turns out that the whack-a-mole approach to auto repair is neither a long-term solution nor a particularly sophisticated diagnosis. Hitting things with a ratchet can work for a time, but after a while you need to take care of your car with a little more precision.

Caring Enough to Be Careful

I'm glad there are people in the world—most people in the world, it turns out—who know more about cars than I do. I don't want good-natured well-wishers to replace my alternator. I want someone who has paid careful attention to the intricacies of auto repair. I want someone who cares about precision. I want someone who knows what he's doing. I want an expert.

To act as if no one knows more than anyone else is not only silly; it's also a serious mistake. In his book *The Death of Expertise*, Tom Nichols cites a survey from a few years ago in which enthusiasm for military intervention in Ukraine was directly proportional to the person's *lack of knowledge* about Ukraine. It seems that the dumber we are, the more confident we are in our own intellectual achievements. Nichols relays an incident where someone on Twitter was trying to do research about sarin gas. When the world's expert on sarin gas offered to help, the original tweeter (a world-class "twit" we might say) proceeded to angrily lecture the expert for acting like a know-it-all. The expert may not have known it all, but in this case, he knew exponentially more than someone crowdsourcing his research online. And when it comes to chemical warfare, I'd like my experts to have as much expertise as possible.

We've swallowed the lie that says that if we believe in equal rights, we must believe that all opinions have equal merit. Nichols also tells the story of an undergraduate student arguing with a renowned astrophysicist who was on campus to give a lecture about missile defense. After seeing that the famous scientist was not going to change his mind after hearing the arguments from a college sophomore, the student concluded in a harrumph, "Well, your guess is as good as mine." At which point the astrophysicist quickly interjected, "No, no, no. My guesses are much, *much* better than yours."[1] There was nothing wrong with the student asking hard questions, or even getting into an argument. The problem was in assuming he had as much to offer on the subject after a few minutes of reflection as the scientist did after decades of training and research.

We live in an age where passion is often considered an adequate substitute for precision. Charles Spurgeon once advised young ministers that when drawn into controversy, they should "use very hard arguments and very soft words."[2] It's a good thing Spurgeon never used social media! Too many tweets and posts specialize in overly hard words and especially soft arguments. Many of us, even Christians, have little patience for rigorous thinking and little interest in careful definition. We emote better than we reason, and we describe our feelings better than we define our words, which is one reason we need to study old confessions written by dead people. Whatever errors of harshness or exaggerated rhetoric may have existed in earlier centuries of theological discourse, this much is wonderfully and refreshingly true: they were relentlessly

1. Tom Nichols, *The Death of Expertise: The Campaign against Established Knowledge and Why It Matters* (Oxford, UK: Oxford University Press, 2017), 82–83.

2. C. H. Spurgeon, *Lectures to My Students, Complete and Unabridged* (Grand Rapids, MI: Zondervan, 1979), 173.

passionate about doctrinal truth. They cared about biblical fidelity. They cared about definitions. And they cared about precision. Praise God, they cared enough to be careful.

And in no Reformation-era confession or catechism do we see this so clearly as in the Canons of Dort.

A Flower by Any Other Name

If the Canons of Dort are known at all, they are usually known as the progenitor of TULIP—that catchy acronym that summarizes the "Five Points of Calvinism." Growing up in a Dutch Reformed church, I remember learning as a child that we believed in Total Depravity, Unconditional Election, Limited Atonement, Irresistible Grace, and Perseverance of the Saints. I'm thankful for this handy summary of key soteriological themes. Like any good Dutchman, I've been in many Tulip Time parades and have no desire to banish the TULIP from our theological vocabulary.

And yet for all that TULIP gets right in terms of biblical truth, there are several things that the acronym—or at least the use of it—can get wrong.

First, TULIP is not an adequate summary of Calvinism. Calvinism was never limited to predestination. In fact, it's not even fair to say predestination was at the heart of Calvin's theology. Cleary, we know from Dort itself that the doctrine is important to Reformed theology, but we should not limit Calvinism to soteriological concerns alone. Reformed theology is not less than the doctrine of salvation and the so-called doctrines of grace, but it is much more.[3]

---

3. Although the term *Calvinism* is not, from the historian's perspective, the best shorthand description for a broad movement of theologians and centuries of theological development, it has become virtually synonymous with the Reformed confessional tradition and thus will be used in this work interchangeably with the word *Reformed*. Whether those who affirm Dort's soteriology but reject important parts of the Reformed tradition can still be called Calvinists is an issue that continues to divide both academic historians and contemporary practitioners.

Second, TULIP is not a historic summary of Calvinism. Although the Canons of Dort have five points, like TULIP has five points, the latter was not used to summarize the former until the twentieth century. The acronym was popularized by David Steele and Curtis Thomas in their 1963 book *The Five Points of Calvinism: Defined, Defended, Documented*.[4] Fifty years earlier, we have the earliest known use of TULIP in a 1913 periodical called *The Outlook*. This doesn't mean we shouldn't talk about the doctrines contained in TULIP, but it does mean we shouldn't oversell the acronym as the best or the only way to talk about the Canons of Dort, let alone talk about Calvinism as a whole.[5]

Third, TULIP is not an entirely accurate summary of the canons themselves. As we will see in the chapters ahead, the Canons of Dort, even with five points, cannot be reduced to only five theological truths. The canons are more detailed, more comprehensive, and more nuanced than can be captured in TULIP. In short, although we don't have to get rid of the acronym, we should appreciate that there are many more flowers in the Dort garden than just the TULIP.

What Arminius Hath Wrought

Before we explore *what* the canons say, we have to understand *why* they say what they do. In other words, we need some history before we get to theology.[6] And that means we have to know how people who once thought of themselves as Calvinists

---

4. David N. Steele and Curtis C. Thomas, *The Five Points of Calvinism: Defined, Defended, Documented* (Phillipsburg, NJ: Presbyterian & Reformed, 1963).

5. See Kenneth J. Stewart, *Ten Myths about Calvinism: Recovering the Breadth of the Reformed Tradition* (Downers Grove, IL: IVP Academic, 2011), 75–95.

6. My historical summary is a distillation of three works: *Crisis in the Reformed Churches: Essays in Commemoration of the Great Synod of Dort, 1618–1619*, ed. Peter Y. De Jong (repr. Grandville, MI: Reformed Fellowship, 2008), 17–71; Matthew Barrett, *The Grace of Godliness: An Introduction to Doctrine and Piety in the Canons of Dort* (Kitchener, Ontario: Joshua Press, 2013), 9–22; Cornelis P. Venema, *But for the Grace of God: An Exposition of the Canons of Dort* (repr. Grandville, MI: Reformed Fellowship, 2016), 10–19.

came to be known as Arminians. The history can seem a little dense, what with strange Dutch places and stranger Dutch names (even though my parents always taught me "if you ain't Dutch, you ain't much!"). Some people get tripped up from the very beginning, misplacing the *i* in Arminian for an *e* (trust me, the historical debate has nothing to do with Armenians from Western Asia). So before setting out on this brief historical journey, perhaps it would be helpful to get a rundown of both teams. The traditional Calvinists (Reformed) are on the left and the Arminians are on the right.

Reformed: The Christians and churches in sixteenth- and seventeenth-century Europe that held to one or more of the Reformed confessions. In the Netherlands this meant the Belgic Confession (1561) and the Heidelberg Catechism (1563). The Canons of Dort were later added to these two documents and together became known as the Three Forms of Unity. I sometimes refer to the Reformed in this book as traditional Calvinists.

Arminians: Initially, these were the followers of Jacob Arminius, but Arminian theology continued to develop after his death in 1609. Later Arminians like John and Charles Wesley (or your Methodist or Free Will Baptist friend next door) probably bear some theological resemblance to the Arminians at Dort, but we should not assume a one-to-one correspondence. As Arminianism developed in Europe in the seventeenth century, it became more and more heterodox.

Counter Remonstrants: The Reformed party in the Netherlands opposed to the Arminians.

Remonstrants: The Arminian party in the Netherlands, so called because of the protest document they issued called the *Remonstrance of 1610*.

John Calvin (1509–1564): Genevan Reformer and one of the most important pastors and theologians in the development of the Reformed tradition.

Jacobus Arminius (1560–1609): Pastor and later professor at the University of Leiden who came to reject traditional Reformed doctrines.

Theodore Beza (1519–1605): Scholar, Reformer, and successor to Calvin in Geneva.

Dirk Volkertszoon Coornhert (1522–1590): Dutch theologian who opposed the teachings of Theodore Beza.

Francis Gomarus (1563–1641): Professor at the University of Leiden who opposed Arminius. The Counter Remonstrants were sometimes called Gomarists.

Prince Maurice (1567–1625): Son of William of Orange; organized successful Dutch rebellion against Spain; national leader in the Netherlands who sided with the Gomarists.

Gisbertus Voetius (1589–1676): Studied theology under Gomarus; delegate at Dort; later professor at the University of Utrecht for forty-two years; leading Dutch theologian of the seventeenth century.

Johannes Bogerman (1576–1637): Pastor and scholar who served as president of the Synod of Dort and helped translate the Scriptures into Dutch.

Canons of Dort (1619): The doctrinal pronouncements from the Synod of Dort, organized under five main points of doctrine.

Johannes Uytenbogaert (1557–1644): Preacher at The Hague; assumed leadership of the Remonstrants after Arminius's death.

Johan van Oldenbarneveldt (1547–1619): Longtime political leader in the Netherlands who sided with the Remonstrants; was executed on May 13, 1619.

Conrad Vorstius (1569–1622): Professor at the University of Leiden whose Arminian views veered off into heterodoxy; was banished from the Netherlands when he refused to recant.

Simon Episcopius (1583–1643): Professor at the University of Leiden; chief spokesman for the Remonstrants; argued that Christianity was more a life than a doctrine.

Opinions of the Remonstrants (1618): The opinions (sometimes called the *Sententia*) offered by the Arminians at the Synod of Dort.

Those are some of the most important names in the story. So how exactly did the story unfold?

Jacobus Arminius lived from 1560–1609, just barely overlapping with John Calvin, who died in 1564. Arminius began his teaching career thoroughly Calvinistic. After studying for a time in Geneva (1582–1587) under Calvin's successor, Theodore Beza, Arminius moved to Amsterdam to pastor a prominent church. As a pastor, Arminius was called upon to defend the views of his former teacher against the attacks of a Dutch theologian named Dirk Volkertszoon Coornhert (1522–1590). In preparing his defense of traditional Calvinist doctrine, Arminius became convinced of his opponent's teaching. Later, Arminius preached a series of sermons on Romans in which he emphasized free will and stressed the government's authority in ecclesiastical and religious matters. Many began to doubt whether Arminius was really in line with the doctrinal standards of the Dutch church: the Heidelberg Catechism and the Belgic Confession (especially Article 16 on the doctrine of election).

In 1603 Arminius was appointed professor of theology at the University of Leiden, where he was strongly opposed by his colleague Francis Gomarus. Both Arminius and Gomarus believed in predestination, but they differed over the meaning of the word. At the heart of the disagreement was whether predestination is based solely on the will of God (traditional Calvinism) or on foreseen knowledge of belief. In 1608 Arminius and Gomarus met for a public debate, but the issue was no closer to being settled. Both men thought of themselves as Reformed, but they were not saying the same thing.

Following Arminius's death in 1609, the movement continued under the leadership of Johannes Uytenbogaert, a court preacher at The Hague. In 1610, the Arminians met at Gouda (sort of a cheesy place for a theological convocation) and issued a document called the *Remonstrance*, setting forth "The Five Arminian Articles."[7] A remonstrance is a protestation, or the reasons given for a statement of opposition. Because of this document, and because the Arminians disagreed with Reformed theology as it was understood and practiced in the Netherlands, they became known as the Remonstrants. The only reason we have the five points of Calvinism is that the Arminians first had their five points. Because the points are at times deliberately ambiguous, and other times

---

7. I will be using the Remonstrance of 1610 as found in De Jong, *Crisis in the Reformed Churches*, 243–45.

highly nuanced, it can be difficult to see what the fuss was all about. In fact, most people reading the Remonstrance of 1610 today would be hard pressed to spot the subtle but important distinctions between the Arminians and the traditional Calvinists.

- Point 1 affirms that God "determined before the foundation of the world to save out of the fallen sinful human race those in Christ, for Christ's sake, and through Christ who by the grace of the Holy Spirit shall believe in this his Son Jesus Christ." That sounds like Ephesians 1, except that it's not clear on what basis God determines the elect. Does God choose the elect so that they might believe in Jesus Christ, or does he choose the elect based on foreseen knowledge that they shall believe in Jesus Christ? We know from the arguments at the Synod of Dort that the Arminians clearly meant the latter.

- According to point 2, Jesus Christ "died for all men and for every man, so that he merited reconciliation and forgiveness of sins for all through the death of the cross; yet so that no one actually enjoys this forgiveness of sins except the believer." Here we can see the conflict with what Dort would teach concerning "limited atonement." The Arminians believed that Christ merited forgiveness for every human being, but that this procured salvation is only effective in those who believe.

- At first glance, point 3 sounds a lot like total depravity, with the Arminians affirming that "man does not have saving faith of himself nor by the power of his own free will." Moreover, they teach that we cannot do anything truly good without first being regenerated through the Holy Spirit and renewed in all powers. The rub is that the Remonstrance does not make clear whether this spiritual inability is a death or a sickness and whether the remedy is a monergistic (one-work-working) resurrection or a grace-filled, cooperative empowerment.

- We see in point 4 that Arminian grace was not sovereign grace as traditional Reformed theology had understood it, but rather a "prevenient or assisting, awakening, consequent and cooperating grace." The Remonstrants certainly believed in grace. They affirmed that all our good works must be "ascribed to the grace of God in Christ." But this was a coming-alongside grace instead of a unilaterally-bring-you-back-from-the-dead grace. Prevenient grace is the grace that comes before human decision and makes it possible (but not certain) for men and women to choose God. For this reason, the Arminians denied that saving grace is "irresistible."

- Point 5 teaches that "those who are incorporated into Jesus Christ" have "abundant strength to strive against Satan, sin, and the world," and that in this struggle the believers are helped by Christ and by "the assistance of the grace of the Holy Spirit." But there is an "if" to this perseverance. Jesus Christ assists believers through his Spirit "if only they are prepared for warfare and desire his help and are not negligent." In the end, the *Remonstrance of 1610* left the door open that believers might "through negligence fall away from the principle of their life in Christ" and "again embrace the present world."

In response to the *Remonstrance of 1610*, Gomarus and others formed a Counter Remonstrant party (sometimes called the Gomarists) to oppose the Arminians. Representatives from both sides met in the spring of that year to see if their differences could be resolved. With the publication of the *Counter Remonstrance* in 1611, it was increasingly clear to everyone involved that the two sides were only getting farther apart. The controversy further escalated when the University of Leiden appointed Arminius's successor—a man by the name of Conrad Vorstius, who was not only an Arminian but practically a Socinian. When the Arminian Simon Episcopius was named as Gomarus's replacement at Leiden, and the Arminians garnered further support from the statesman Johan van Oldenbarneveldt and the jurist-theologian Hugo Grotius, it looked like the tide had turned in favor of the Remonstrants.

As with many theological controversies throughout history, the disputing factions were disputing about more than just theology. The Netherlands had recently won independence from Spain. Some were still leery of the Spanish, while others welcomed a closer relationship. In general, the merchant class, for economic and trading reasons, desired improved relations with Spain. The clergy, on the other hand, feared that more contact with Catholic Spain would taint the theology of their churches. The lower class sided with the clergy for theological reasons, for national reasons (anti-Spain), and for class reasons (anti-merchants). Thus, the merchants saw Arminianism as favorable to their desire for improved relations with Spain, while the clergy and lower class sided with Gomarus.

In 1617 Oldenbarneveldt and the States General issued the "Sharp Resolution," rejecting the call for a national synod. Oldenbarneveldt was heralded by some as a champion of toleration, but the party of the Counter Remonstrant worried that without a national synod and with States General exercising control over ecclesiastical matters (including the authorization of soldiers to defend the Remonstrants) the conflict was only going to get worse.

That same year, the Reformed Prince Maurice, the son and heir of the beloved William of Orange, refused to worship in the church because Uytenbogaert was preaching. Oldenbarneveldt threatened civil war, which led to his arrest by Maurice. In response, a number of the Remonstrants fled the country, and with Maurice now in charge, the States General finally approved the calling of a national assembly to address the conflict.

The Synod

Although the controversy had national and political overtones, at heart it was an earnest theological disagreement. The differences centered on the doctrine of predestination, but confessional subscription was also a major part of the dispute, with the Remonstrants arguing for full doctrinal freedom and the Counter Remonstrants insisting that the Dutch church was a confessional church that ought to preserve theological unity and purity in the pulpit. So for the first time since 1586, the Dutch government called for a national synod, this time in the city of Dordrecht.[8]

The synod met from November 13, 1618, until May 29, 1619. Of the eighty-four members present, twenty-six were from Britain, Switzerland, and Germany, while the rest were Dutch.[9] The Dutch contingent was comprised of roughly an equal number of ministers, professors, laymen, and members of the States General. On Friday morning, November 16, the synod voted to call the Remonstrants to appear before the assembly within two weeks. On December 13 and 17, the Arminians presented *The Opinions of the Remonstrants* (also called the *Sententia*), which are crucial

---

8. Of personal interest to me (and perhaps to no one else) is that my family descends from Dordrecht. I'd like to think I had a family member in attendance at the synod (hopefully on the right side!). The earliest ancestor that has been traced in my family tree is Pieter DeJong, who was born in Dordrecht in 1695 and married Neeltje Liesveld of neighboring Zwijndrecht on August 23, 1716. The first of my family to emigrate to America was Teunis P. DeJong, who was born in Holland in 1839, died in Edgerton, Minnesota, in 1925, and was married to Cornelia VanDeursen in Keokuk, Iowa, in 1861. According to family tradition, "DeJong" became "DeYoung" when Teunis (or one of his relatives?) registered to fight for the Union in the Civil War and his name was recorded with the Anglicized spelling.

9. Two delegates, Johannes Bergius and Christoph Storch from Brandenburg, were unable to come because of Lutheran opposition. An additional four delegates from France were never granted permission to the leave the country. Their four seats were left open during the synod in their honor.

for understanding what Dort was aiming to criticize and correct (see Appendix 3).

By January, the Arminians were dismissed from the synod by president Johannes Bogerman for their failure to cooperate with the proceedings. Around the same time, the States General granted the synod official status as an ecclesiastical court, and by the end of March all the written opinions of the delegates had been reviewed. On April 22, 1619, the synod adopted the canons and settled, for the Netherlands and for all subsequent churches that would adopt the canons as their own, what constituted authentic Reformed faith on the points of disputed theology. The Canons of Dort were published in an official Latin edition on May 6, 1619, with approved translations into Dutch and French. In addition to the Canons, the synod also approved an official edition of the Belgic Confession, adopted a church order, and commissioned a new Dutch translation of the Bible.

The Canons of Dort, in rejecting the five points of Arminianism, outlined five points of their own. The first concerned divine election and reprobation; the second was on Christ's death and human redemption through it; the third and fourth points were on human corruption and how we convert to God; and a final point focused on the perseverance of the saints. The canons do not pretend to explain everything about Reformed theology, let alone about the entire Bible. Dort simply sought to declare what was "in agreement with the Word of God and accepted till now in the Reformed churches" concerning "Divine Predestination." And in this they are worthy to be commemorated and (more importantly) deserving of careful study and consideration.

Letting Grace Be Grace

It's easy to think that the two sides in the Netherlands should have found a way to work out their differences. Oldenbarneveldt was ready to go to civil war over the religious dispute, while Maurice, sadly, ended up condemning Oldenbarneveldt to death and had some Arminian pastors imprisoned. We cringe to see political meddling in the name of theology, not to mention the threat of violence and imprisonment that marked both sides as people of their time. But if we don't care about theological precision and definition, it's not because we are so wonderfully inclusive and loving, as much as it is that we too are people of our own time. We settle for generalities and ambiguities and wonder why anyone should demand anything more.

The stereotype of old confessions like the Canons of Dort is that they take the theology of God's Word and make it shrink-wrapped, freeze-dried, and boxed-up. Or, if we can mix our metaphors, theologizing becomes nothing more than dissecting a dead frog.

But what if another analogy is more appropriate? What if the truth we are talking about is not cold and dead, but very much alive? What if, instead of thinking about dissecting a frog, you think about defining or defending your child? If someone mistook your child for someone else, or if someone ran off with your child, you would care very much about definitions. You would want people to know the name of your child. It wouldn't be enough to just say, "I'm looking for a cute kid out there. Just bring me one." You would be precise about her name, her height, her hair, her eyes, and her voice. You would provide a careful definition of your child. Likewise, if someone misunderstood your child or attacked your child, wouldn't you do everything in your power to defend him? Of course you would, because your child is *precious*.

And so it is with the truth of God's Word. Before the Synod of Dort conducted its business, each member took a solemn oath saying that "I will only aim at the glory of God, the peace of the Church, and especially the preservation of the purity of doctrine."

They ended with a prayer: "So help me, my Savior, Jesus Christ! I beseech him to assist me by his Holy Spirit."[10] The delegates at Dort were joyfully serious about the doctrine of the church.

Do we care as much about defining and defending grace?

In Romans 11, Paul argues that there is a "remnant, chosen by grace" (v. 5). He then moves to defend and define this grace, maintaining that "if it is by grace, it is no longer on the basis of works; otherwise grace would no longer be grace" (v. 6). Words mattered to Paul. He was never content to casually speak the same vocabulary as his opponents, if he knew they were using different dictionaries. He understood that people can champion grace, laud grace, and celebrate grace, while still losing all that makes grace grace.

At their very heart, the Canons of Dort are about the nature of grace—supernatural, unilateral, sovereign, effecting, redeeming, resurrecting grace, with all of its angularity, all of its offense to human pride, and all of its comfort for the weary soul. That's what Dort wanted to settle. That's what they were jealous to protect. Some words are worth the most careful definitions, just as some truths are too precious not to defend.

---

10. Quoted by Fred Klooster, "Doctrinal Deliverances of Dort," in DeJong, *Crisis in the Reformed Churches*, 79. In the rest of the oath, the members of the synod promise before God to settle the dispute over the five points using only the Bible.

1

God's Purpose and Good Pleasure in Predestination

The First Main Point of Doctrine

I took AP Western Civilization when I was in high school. I've forgotten a lot since then, but I vividly remember the class where we talked about the Reformation. Even though it was a public high school, my teacher found a way to get us talking about Luther and Calvin. In discussing Calvin, we couldn't avoid a heated conversation about predestination.

The class uniformly thought the idea of God choosing people for salvation was ghastly. But I remembered my mom telling me that "we like John Calvin," so I felt duty bound to put in a good word for the Genevan Reformer. I raised my hand and, once called upon, explained to my classmates that predestination simply meant that God looked into the future to see who would believe, and then God elected those people for salvation. To my delight, the class seemed quite satisfied with my explanation. To think that God chose those whom he knew would choose him was a much easier pill to swallow. Only years later did I realize that I had magnificently defended Calvinism with Arminianism!

The First Main Point of Doctrine in Dort is the longest and the most theologically complicated. But at the heart of the debate is a straightforward question: Did God choose the elect *because* they would believe, or did God choose the elect *so that* they might believe? Or to put it another way, is divine election based on foreseen faith or according to sheer grace and God's free good pleasure? That's what Dort's first point means to answer.

Two Quick Notes

Before we turn to the canons themselves, I need to make two brief introductory remarks.

1. This book is not a biblical defense of the five points of Calvinism, nor is it a theological exposition of Reformed soteriology. There are a number of good books that set out to do one or both of those tasks.[1] While I trust this book will also be biblical and theological (see Appendix 4 for all of Dort's Scripture proofs), my first goal is to explain the Canons of Dort. Think of this not as a mini systematic theology or as an exegetical exploration of key salvation texts, but as a brief, accessible commentary on the background and theology of Dort itself. Of course, in explaining Dort, I hope to say something valuable about the theology of the Bible as well. But you can be the judge of that.

2. When referencing or quoting from the canons, I will put the article in parentheses. Since each of these references will be for the main point of doctrine under consideration, I'll note the

---

1. R. C. Sproul, *What Is Reformed Theology: Understanding the Basics* (Grand Rapids, MI: Baker, 1997); David N. Steele, Curtis C. Thomas, S. Lance Quinn, *The Five Points of Calvinism: Defined, Defended, Documented* (Phillipsburg, NJ: P&R, 2004); Michael Horton, *For Calvinism* (Grand Rapids, MI: Zondervan, 2011); John Piper, *Five Points: Towards a Deeper Experience of God's Grace* (Ross-Shire, UK: Christian Focus, 2013).

article number only. Besides the articles provided in the text of each chapter, the canons also include a section called "Rejection of Errors" after each main point of doctrine. These rejections can be found in Appendix 1. I will cite these parenthetically, so that (Rejection III) refers to the third rejection for the main point under discussion. There is a concluding section entitled "Rejection of False Accusations" included in Appendix 2. Finally, *The Opinions of the Remonstrants* can be found in Appendix 3. These will be referenced as (*Opinions* C.3) or (*Opinions* A.9) and so on.[2]

Framing the Debate (Articles 1–5)

Article 1: God's Right to Condemn All People

Since all people have sinned in Adam and have come under the sentence of the curse and eternal death, God would have done no one an injustice if it had been his will to leave the entire human race in sin and under the curse, and to condemn them on account of their sin. As the apostle says: "The whole world is liable to the condemnation of God" (Rom. 3:19), "All have sinned and are deprived of the glory of God" (Rom. 3:23), and "The wages of sin is death" (Rom. 6:23).

Article 2: The Manifestation of God's Love

But this is how God showed his love: he sent his only begotten Son into the world, so that whoever believes in him should not perish but have eternal life (1 John 4:9; John 3:16).

Article 3: The Preaching of the Gospel

In order that people may be brought to faith, God mercifully sends messengers of this very joyful message to the people and

---

2. The *Opinions* are taken from *Crisis in the Reformed Churches: Essays in Commemoration of the Great Synod of Dort, 1618–1619*, ed. Peter Y. De Jong (repr. Grandville, MI: Reformed Fellowship, 2008), 261–68. The text for the Canons of Dort, including the Rejection of Errors and the Rejection of False Accusations, is the translation approved by the Christian Reformed Church.

at the time he wills. By this ministry people are called to repentance and faith in Christ crucified. For "how shall they believe in him of whom they have not heard? And how shall they hear without someone preaching? And how shall they preach unless they have been sent?" (Rom. 10:14–15).

Article 4: A Twofold Response to the Gospel

God's wrath remains on those who do not believe this gospel. But those who do accept it and embrace Jesus the Savior with a true and living faith are delivered through him from God's wrath and from destruction, and receive the gift of eternal life.

Article 5: The Sources of Unbelief and of Faith

The cause or blame for this unbelief, as well as for all other sins, is not at all in God, but in humanity. Faith in Jesus Christ, however, and salvation through him is a free gift of God. As Scripture says, "It is by grace you have been saved, through faith, and this not from yourselves; it is a gift of God" (Eph. 2:8). Likewise: "It has been freely given to you to believe in Christ" (Phil. 1:29).

✳ ✳ ✳

These first five articles are essential for understanding the rest of this First Main Point and for putting all of the canons in a proper biblical framework.

At the outset, before even talking about election unto salvation, we have to accept that "God would have done no one an injustice if it had been his will to leave the entire human race in sin and under the curse, and to condemn them on account of their sin" (Article 1). The question is not simply, "Why do *some* people get passed over?" but, "Why should *anyone* be saved?" We are all deserving of punishment and death. It is only by God's grace that any of us receive eternal life.

Because God loves us, he sent two great gifts into the world. The supreme gift was the sending of his Son so that whoever believes in him should not perish but have eternal life (Article 2). The other gift mentioned here by Dort is the sending of messengers to proclaim this good news (Article 3). As we'll see again, the doctrine of predestination does not eliminate the need for faithful preachers and evangelists. God normally works through means, which means he saves his people through the preaching of the gospel (Acts 18:9–11; 2 Thess. 2:13–14).

Most Christians would agree with everything in Articles 1–3. There is nothing too controversial (for orthodox believers) about sinners deserving death, God showing love, and preachers proclaiming the gospel. And among Bible-believing Christians, there is nothing much to debate when it comes to Article 4: whoever believes in Christ is not condemned, but whoever does not believe is condemned already (John 3:18).

By the time we get to Article 5, however, Dort is setting us up for the crux of the matter. Some people believe, and some people do not. That much is self-evident. We can all see this. Further, as Christians, we probably all agree that unbelief is our fault, while salvation is the free gift of God. Following the Bible, Dort has divided humanity into two classes: those who are lost (because of sin) and those who are found (because of grace). This much we can all (for the most part) agree on.

Election Defined (Articles 6–11)

Article 6: God's Eternal Decree

The fact that some receive from God the gift of faith within time, and that others do not, stems from his eternal decree. For "all his works are known to God from eternity" (Acts 15:18;

Eph. 1:11). In accordance with this decree God graciously softens the hearts, however hard, of the elect and inclines them to believe, but by a just judgment God leaves in their wickedness and hardness of heart those who have not been chosen. And in this especially is disclosed to us God's act—unfathomable, and as merciful as it is just—of distinguishing between people equally lost. This is the well-known decree of election and reprobation revealed in God's Word. The wicked, impure, and unstable distort this decree to their own ruin, but it provides holy and godly souls with comfort beyond words.

Article 7: Election

Election is God's unchangeable purpose by which he did the following:

Before the foundation of the world, by sheer grace, according to the free good pleasure of his will, God chose in Christ to salvation a definite number of particular people out of the entire human race, which had fallen by its own fault from its original innocence into sin and ruin. Those chosen were neither better nor more deserving than the others, but lay with them in the common misery. God did this in Christ, whom he also appointed from eternity to be the Mediator, the head of all those chosen, and the foundation of their salvation.

And so God decreed to give to Christ those chosen for salvation, and to call and draw them effectively into Christ's fellowship through the Word and Spirit. In other words, God decreed to grant them true faith in Christ, to justify them, to sanctify them, and finally, after powerfully preserving them in the fellowship of the Son, to glorify them.

God did all this in order to demonstrate his mercy, to the praise of the riches of God's glorious grace. As Scripture says,

"God chose us in Christ, before the foundation of the world, so that we should be holy and blameless before him with love; he predestined us whom he adopted as his children through Jesus Christ, in himself, according to the good pleasure of his will, to the praise of his glorious grace, by which he freely made us pleasing to himself in his beloved" (Eph. 1:4–6). And elsewhere, "Those whom he predestined, he also called; and those whom he called, he also justified; and those whom he justified, he also glorified" (Rom. 8:30).

Article 8: A Single Decree of Election

This election is not of many kinds, but one and the same for all who were to be saved in the Old and the New Testament. For Scripture declares that there is a single good pleasure, purpose, and plan of God's will, by which he chose us from eternity both to grace and to glory, both to salvation and to the way of salvation, which God prepared in advance for us to walk in.

Article 9: Election Not Based on Foreseen Faith

This same election took place, not on the basis of foreseen faith, of the obedience of faith, of holiness, or of any other good quality and disposition, as though it were based on a prerequisite cause or condition in the person to be chosen, but rather for the purpose of faith, of the obedience of faith, of holiness, and so on. Accordingly, election is the source of every saving good. Faith, holiness, and the other saving gifts, and at last eternal life itself, flow forth from election as its fruits and effects. As the apostle says, "He chose us" [not because we were [holy], but] "so that we should be holy and blameless before him in love" (Eph. 1:4).

Article 10: Election Based on God's Good Pleasure

But the cause of this undeserved election is exclusively the good pleasure of God. This does not involve God's choosing certain human qualities or actions from among all those possible as a condition of salvation, but rather involves adopting certain particular persons from among the common mass of sinners as God's own possession. As Scripture says, "When the children were not yet born, and had done nothing either good or bad . . . she [Rebecca] was told, 'The older will serve the younger.' As it is written, 'Jacob I loved, but Esau I hated'" (Rom. 9:11–13). Also, "All who were appointed for eternal life believed" (Acts 13:48).

Article 11: Election Unchangeable

Just as God is most wise, unchangeable, all-knowing, and almighty, so the election made by him can neither be suspended nor altered, revoked, or annulled; neither can God's chosen ones be cast off, nor their number reduced.

✳ ✳ ✳

After explaining the *what* of judgment, gospel, and grace, Dort now brings us to the *why*. We can all see that some people believe in Christ and others do not. But why? What is the ultimate reason that some exercise faith, while others remain in unbelief? There are really only two possible answers: God or man. After we talk about proximate causes like families of origin and cultural factors and all the rest, the *ultimate* reason why some believe (and others do not) must rest with either man's determination or God's divine plan.

The answer, according to Article 6, is on the side of divine decision. "The fact that some receive from God the gift of faith within time, and that others do not, stems from his eternal decree." As this decree is executed in time, God softens the hearts of the elect and inclines them to believe, while he leaves the reprobate in their wickedness. Notice that for Dort, the decree of election and reprobation concerns "people equally lost." Out of this mass (and mess) of human sinners, God freely chose some for salvation and freely passed by others to leave them in their deserved misery.

That is the doctrine of election in summary form, but we must pay attention to several other important definitions and distinctions in Articles 7–11.

First, election is not based on foreseen faith (see Rejection V). God chose us in Christ not *because* he saw that we would be holy and blameless, but *so that* we should be holy and blameless (Eph. 1:4–6). God's decision to choose some for salvation is not based upon any prerequisite cause or condition (Article 9), but only upon sheer grace, according to the good pleasure of his will (Article 7). This is in direct opposition to Arminian position, which stated that the "election of particular persons" is out of "consideration of faith in Jesus Christ and of perseverance" as a "condition prerequisite for electing" (*Opinions* A.7).

Second, election is an unchangeable decree. This may seem self-evident. How could an immutable God decree one thing and then decree the opposite? But the Arminians believed that God could decree certain contingent effects without issuing "a decree of the end absolutely intended" (*Opinions* A.2). In other words, God could will certain ends that may or may not come to pass because his decree did not also include the means to those ends. Against this view, Dort affirms that the election made by an unchangeable God "can neither be suspended nor altered, revoked, or annulled" (Article 11). This is good news: God's elect can never be lost, and their number can never be lessened.

Third, election is a single decree. This is related to the last point. The Arminians believed that election functioned in different ways and on different levels. God might elect some for blessings that are incomplete, revocable, and contingent, while decreeing that other blessings are particular and definite (Rejection II, IV). For example, it was common to speak of God having an antecedent will (what God decreed before he saw who would believe) and a consequent will (what God decreed after he saw who would believe). So according to his antecedent will, God can choose all persons for primordial benevolence, but according to his consequent will, God chooses those who will believe for special benevolence. On the Arminian scheme, then, those who are chosen for salvation based on God's consequent will are not predestinated so much as they are postdestined.

In this way, the Arminians could affirm unconditional election (of a kind) *and* conditional election. Dort wanted to make clear that this is not what the Reformed churches meant by "predestination." In God's "single good pleasure, purpose, and plan," God chose us "from eternity both to grace and to glory, both to salvation and to the way of salvation" (Article 8). That is to say, God didn't decree that believers would be saved unconditionally, while at the same time making the election of those believers conditional upon foreseen faith. The divine decree is single, and the choice of the elect unconditional from start to finish. God does not plan the ends without planning the means.

Fourth, election involves "certain particular persons" (Article 10). This may seem like a strange point to make, but again, it is in distinction to the Arminian notion that election involves God's choosing of certain human qualities or actions that he will bless, rather than God's choosing of certain particular persons to be his treasured possession. Divine election is not just an act of sovereignty; it's an act of grace. God knew us before the foundation of the world. God sets his affection upon us. In love he predestinated us for adoption as sons through Jesus Christ (Eph. 1:4–5). Election is about God choosing *specific* people to save, not about God choosing the *kinds* of people he will save.

Fifth, we must say something about Dort's recurring insistence that God chooses "between people equally lost" (Article 6) or from "among the common mass of sinners" (Article 10). Keep in mind that election takes place in eternity past, from before the foundation of the world. So the distinction "between people equally lost" is made in the will of God, not first in history. This gets us into one of the most intricate debates in Reformed theology: the debate between supralapsarianism and infralapsarianism.

Theologians have often argued about the order in which God decreed certain things to happen. The debate is not over the *temporal* order of the decrees. After all, we are talking about what God has determined in eternity, before he created the world with time (which is why, strictly speaking, eternity *past* is not quite the right phrase). Time is not the issue. In fact, time as a sequential ordering of events cannot even be predicated of God. Instead, the debate is about the *logical* order of the decrees. In the mind of God, what is the object of God's decree: man with the potential to fall (*homo labilis*) or man as fallen (*homo lapsum*)?

Or to put it another way, which is logically prior: the decree of election and reprobation, or the decree to create the world and permit the fall? Supralapsarianism—*supra* meaning "above" or "before" and *lapsum* meaning "fall"—is the position that holds that God's decree to save is logically *prior* to his decree to create the world and permit the fall. Infralapsarianism, on the other hand, insists that God's decree to save is logically *after* his decrees related to creation and fall (*infra* meaning "below" or "after"). Both positions are well attested in Reformed theology, though infralapsarianism would probably be more common.

The Canons of Dort work from infralapsarian principles, arguing several times that God's decree of election is logically below or after (*infra*) the fall. Hence, election is God's choice to save fallen sinners from destruction, and reprobation is God's choice to leave fallen sinners in their plight. Of course, the theologians at Dort would also have affirmed that the fall too was part of God's plan. But according to Dort's logic, divine election was a choice to save sinners, not a choice to save people who need to sin first in order to be saved. After all, Romans 9:14 describes election as God having *mercy* on whom he will have mercy. God's decree to save, therefore, must follow his decree to permit the fall, or how else would mercy be mercy?

Assurance Found (Articles 12–13)

Article 12: The Assurance of Election

Assurance of their eternal and unchangeable election to salvation is given to the chosen in due time, though by various stages and in differing measure. Such assurance comes not by inquisitive searching into the hidden and deep things of God, but by noticing within themselves, with spiritual joy and holy delight, the unmistakable fruits of election pointed out in God's Word—such as a true faith in Christ, a childlike fear of God, a godly sorrow for their sins, a hunger and thirst for righteousness, and so on.

Article 13: The Fruit of This Assurance

In their awareness and assurance of this election, God's children daily find greater cause to humble themselves before God, to adore the fathomless depth of God's mercies, to cleanse themselves, and to give fervent love in return to the One who first so greatly loved them. This is far from saying that this teaching concerning election, and reflection upon it, make God's children lax in observing his commandments or carnally self-assured. By God's just judgment, this does usually happen to those who casually take for granted the grace of election or engage in idle and brazen talk about it but are unwilling to walk in the ways of the chosen.

❄ ❄ ❄

Although the Canons of Dort are rigorously careful and theologically precise, this does not mean they are pastorally irrelevant. In fact, the driving force behind all their definition and all their defending was a desire to help struggling Christians. Thus, the doctrine of election was for assurance, not for anxiety. Dort rejected those who taught "that in this life there is no fruit, no awareness, and no assurance of one's unchangeable election to glory" (Rejection VII). The members of the synod understood that, wrongly understood, predestination can make people nervous about their eternal state. That's why they warned against "inquisitive searching into the hidden and deep things of God" (Article 12). Confidence in our election is not found by rummaging around the decrees from eternity past. Instead, we ought to look for "the unmistakable fruits of this election"—true faith, childlike fear, godly sorrow for sin, and a hunger and thirst for righteousness (Article 12).

Similarly, Dort is careful to guard against the sinful appropriation of election and reprobation. Election does not mean we are better and worthier people (see Rejection IX). The doctrine is for humility, not for haughtiness. If God chose us, out of the sinful mass of humanity, apart from anything good we had done or any foreknowledge of good we would do, how can we be proud? Likewise, how can we be "lax" or "carnally self-assured" (Article 13)? When we really understand the grace of God in election it makes us humble before God, confident in the face of trials, fervent in love for one another, and steadfast in obedience to the divine law. There should be no such thing as Reformed jerks and proud Calvinists.

Handling Holy Things (Articles 14–18)

Article 14: Teaching Election Properly

By God's wise plan, this teaching concerning divine election was proclaimed through the prophets, Christ himself, and the apostles, in Old and New Testament times. It was subsequently committed to writing in the Holy Scriptures. So also today in God's church, for which it was specifically intended, this teaching must be set forth with a spirit of discretion, in a godly and holy manner, at the appropriate time and place, without inquisitive searching into the ways of the Most High. This must be done for the glory of God's most holy name, and for the lively comfort of God's people.

Article 15: Reprobation

Moreover, Holy Scripture most especially highlights this eternal and underserved grace of our election and brings it out more clearly for us, in that it further bears witness that not all people have been chosen but that some have not been chosen or have been passed by in God's eternal election—those, that is, concerning whom God, on the basis of his entirely free, most just, irreproachable, and unchangeable good pleasure, made the following decree: to leave them in the common misery into which, by their own fault, they have plunged themselves; not to grant them saving faith and the grace of conversion; but finally to condemn and eternally punish those who have been left in their own ways and under God's just judgment, not only for their unbelief but also for all their other sins, in order to display his justice.

And this is the decree of reprobation, which does not at all make God the author of sin (a blasphemous thought!) but rather its fearful, irreproachable, just judge, and avenger.

Article 16: Responses to the Teaching of Reprobation

Those who do not yet actively experience within themselves a living faith in Christ or an assured confidence of heart, peace of conscience, a zeal for childlike obedience, and a glorying in God through Christ, but who nevertheless use the means by which God has promised to work these things in us—such people ought not to be alarmed at the mention of reprobation, nor to count themselves among the reprobate; rather they ought to continue diligently in the use of the means, to desire fervently a time of more abundant grace, and to wait for it in reverence and humility. On the other hand, those who seriously desire to turn to God, to be pleasing to God alone, and to be delivered from the body of death, but are not yet able to make such progress along the way of godliness and faith as they would like—such people ought much less to stand in fear of the teaching concerning reprobation, since our merciful God has promised not to snuff out a smoldering wick or break a bruised reed (Isa. 42:3). However, those who have forgotten God and their Savior Jesus Christ and have abandoned themselves wholly to the cares of the world and the pleasures of the flesh—such people have every reason to stand in fear of this teaching, as long as they do not seriously turn to God.

Article 17: The Salvation of the Infants of Believers

Since we must make judgments about God's will from his Word, which testifies that the children of believers are holy, not by nature but by virtue of the gracious covenant in which they together with their parents are included, godly parents ought not to doubt the election and salvation of their children whom God calls out of this life in infancy.

Article 18: The Proper Attitude Toward Election and Reprobation

To those who complain about this grace of an undeserved election and about the severity of a just reprobation, we reply with the words of the apostle, "Who are you, O man, to talk back to God?" (Rom. 9:20), and with the words of our Savior, "Have

I no right to do what I want with my own?" (Matt. 20:15). We, however, with reverent adoration of these secret things, cry out with the apostle: "Oh, the depths of the riches both of the wisdom and the knowledge of God! How unsearchable are his judgments, and his ways beyond tracing out! For who has known the mind of the Lord? Or who has been his counselor? Or who has first given to God, that God should repay him? For from him and through him and to him are all things. To him be the glory forever! Amen" (Rom. 11:33–36).

The doctrine of election, especially when combined with its counterpart, reprobation, has always been a difficult doctrine for some Christians to accept. It strikes at assumed notions of human freedom. It undermines presumed ideas of human determination. And it removes from human willing the final decisiveness in our salvation. Consequently, there is usually an apologetic angle when talking about predestination, not in apologizing for what the Bible teaches, but in making sure the common misunderstandings about election are explained and the uncommon benefits celebrated. That's what we have in these final articles: an answer to the charges wrongly levied against the Reformed doctrine of predestination.

With that in mind, let's look at three big themes in these final articles.

First, Dort clarifies what is meant by reprobation. In one sense, reprobation is simply the implied inverse of election. On any view of election (even the Arminian view), some people are singled out for favor. That's what election entails. If God chooses some (and not others), then his decree must concern both the elect and the nonelect. You cannot have one without the other. If your theology has election (of particular persons, in the way Dort understands it), then you must also have reprobation. This is not just logical, but biblical. The potter has the right to make from the same lump of clay some vessels for honorable use and some for dishonorable (Rom. 9:21–23). Some people have been destined to stumble (1 Pet. 2:8) and designated for condemnation (Jude 4). God is sovereign over all people and over all things.

No doubt, reprobation is a difficult doctrine, which is why we must be extra careful to understand what Reformed theologians have (and have not) meant by the doctrine. The caricature is that Calvinists believe that God capriciously chooses to create innocent people so that he might damn them for his glory. If this what Arminians think that Calvinists believe, they should be embarrassed. And if this is what Calvinists think they ought to believe, they should be ashamed. We do not believe that God makes play things just to zap them in the microwave of his judgment.

Dort's doctrine of reprobation is much more nuanced than the caricature allows. Remember that from Dort's perspective we are dealing with people already fallen—not fallen in the unfolding of time (we are dealing with the will of God in eternity past), but fallen in the logical unfolding of the decrees. So reprobation is not the decree to punish innocent people. Reprobation is the divine decision whereby "some have not been chosen or have been passed by in God's eternal election" (Article 15). All of that means that reprobation, as the concluding section on false accusations notes, is not "the cause of unbelief and ungodliness" in the same way that "election is the source and cause of faith and good works."

Traditional Reformed theology distinguishes between two elements in reprobation. First there is preterition (the determination to leave fallen sinners in their wickedness), and then there is condemnation (the determination to punish those who are passed by). This distinction is clearly in view when Dort explains that God leaves people in their common misery—not granting them faith and not granting them the grace of conversion—and then finally sentences them to eternal punishment (Article 15). In other words, God doesn't condemn people for being reprobate. He condemns people for sin and unbelief, from which God, according to his good pleasure and sovereign grace, has purposed to rescue only the elect.

The second theme to note in this last section is Dort's approach to those who die in infancy. From the *Rejection of False Accusations*, we can infer that some charged Reformed theology with a cruelly pessimistic view of deceased children, suggesting that those who die in infancy must be cast into hell as reprobates. But this is not Dort's view. Likely owing to 2 Samuel 12:23–24 where David says he will go to be with his dead son (and then comforted his wife), Dort affirms that "godly parents ought not to doubt the election and salvation of their children whom God calls out of this life in infancy" (Article 17). While Dort is silent on the question of noncovenant children, the canons argue that since the children of at least one believing parent are covenantally holy and set apart (1 Cor. 7:14), we can be confident that God will be their God in death just as he was their covenant God in life.

The third theme concerns the teaching of election and reprobation and our response to it. Dort understands that teaching these doctrines requires "a spirit of discretion" (Article 14). Calvinists in the midst of their "cage stage" who beat people up about election (been there) and try to make people cry with reprobation (done that) are acting not only as immature Christians but as poor Calvinists. Dort acknowledges that these things must be taught "at the appropriate time and place," in a way that promotes God's glory and comforts God's people (Article 14).

Of particular concern is the danger that people hearing of reprobation will wonder if they themselves are reprobate. At the beginning of the twentieth century, Max Weber argued that behind the famed Protestant work ethic were anxious Calvinists striving with all their might to prove they were elect. Weber's thesis has been largely discredited in academic circles, but his theological caricature—Reformed people fearing their reprobation—can live on. But nowhere does Dort, or the Bible for that matter, encourage us to plumb the depths of God's eternal decree. Instead, the logic from Jesus in John 6:37 is: "All that the Father gives me will come to me" (election), *and* "whoever comes to me I will never cast out" (the free offer of the gospel). The doctrine of predestination should never be taught so that people conclude, in despair, that they *cannot* come; the doctrine must be articulated so people conclude that by God's grace they *can* come.

Conclusion

As a precise statement of doctrinal convictions, Dort goes to great lengths to make positive affirmations of the truth and negative rejections of error. This includes errors in their opponents (which they wanted to correct) and errors charged to their account (which they wanted to clarify). In other words, if you want to understand the pastoral heartbeat behind the canons, you have to understand what Dort wanted to defend *and* what Dort wanted to deny.

Here are some of the "false accusations" Dort tries to set straight in its concluding paragraphs:

- The Reformed doctrine of election and reprobation does *not* draw "the minds of people away from all godliness and religion."
- It does *not* make "God the author of sin."
- It does *not* make "people carnally self-assured."
- It does *not* mean "that God predestined and created, by the bare and unqualified choice of his will, without the least regard or consideration of any sin, the greatest part of the world to eternal condemnation."

- It does *not* teach "that many infant children of believers are snatched in their innocence from their mothers' breasts and cruelly cast into hell."

All of these are false inferences from, or false accusations against, the Reformed doctrine of predestination.

So, on the one hand, we must be especially careful in handling such hot (and holy!) doctrines. We do not want people despondent in fatalistic resignation (Article 16). And yet we must not go to the other extreme and bury these truths in hypercautious oblivion. Let's not pretend we are smarter than the Bible. If God revealed these things to us, he did so for our good. He wants to warn those who have forgotten their Maker that they will prove themselves to be reprobate if they do not turn to Christ (Article 16), while at the same time leading the believer to receive these "secret things" with "reverent adoration" (Article 18). When face-to-face with the "grace of an undeserved election and the severity of a just reprobation" we ought to bow in humble submission to the will of God, tell of his unsearchable judgments, and worship the one to whom belongs glory forever and ever (Rom. 11:33–36).

2

Redemption Accomplished *and* Applied

The Second Main Point of Doctrine

The doctrine of limited atonement—or particular redemption or, as I'll call it, definite atonement—is the least affirmed and the most difficult to understand of Dort's five points. It's tempting, therefore, to sideline definite atonement as less important than the other points, or at least less to be argued about and insisted upon. But this would be a mistake. The doctrine of definite atonement is massively important for our theology and for our worship. In fact, I'd argue that definite atonement is so integral to the biblical system taught by Dort that without the *L* in the TULIP, the whole flower withers. For, as we'll see, the doctrine is not just about the *extent* of the atonement but about the *nature* of the atonement. Did the Son of God die to make salvation merely possible or to make people saved? That's the literal crux of the matter.

The debate is not an idiosyncratic bit of theological wrangling. The how and the why of worship are at stake. Bad theology leads to despair, and proud theology leads to disdain. But humble, heartfelt Reformed theology should always lead to doxology. In the last article of this section, we read that the church shaped by definite atonement is "a church which steadfastly loves, persistently worships, and here and in all eternity praises [Christ] as her Savior who laid down his life for her on the cross, as a bridegroom for his bride" (Article 9). Spoiler alert: that's where we are going and that's why definite atonement matters. Yes, we want to get our theology right. But even more, we want to give Christ all the praise he deserves.

Mercy and Justice Meet (Articles 1–2)

Article 1: *The Punishment Which God's Justice Requires*

> God is not only supremely merciful, but also supremely just. This justice requires (as God has revealed in the Word) that the sins we have committed against his infinite majesty be punished with both temporal and eternal punishments, of soul as well as body. We cannot escape these punishments unless satisfaction is given to God's justice.

Article 2: *The Satisfaction Made by Christ*

> Since, however, we ourselves cannot give this satisfaction or deliver ourselves from God's wrath, God in boundless mercy has given us as a guarantee his only begotten Son, who was made to be sin and a curse for us, in our place, on the cross, in order that he might give satisfaction for us.

✳ ✳ ✳

As we saw with the First Main Point of Doctrine, Dort begins by putting the theological controversy in a broader redemptive-historical context. Before we can talk about the nature or the extent of the atonement, we need to remember why atonement is necessary. To that end, Dort grounded the discussion in the need for divine satis-faction. Curiously enough, although Dort's second point is usually referred to as limited or definite atonement, the word *atonement* doesn't appear anywhere in these nine articles. That doesn't mean we are wrong to use the word. It does mean, however, that Dort is not first of all about how estranged parties get reconciled (at-one-ment) but about how God's justice can be satisfied.

This is a critical starting place. Some contemporary Christians see the cross as an expression of self-giving love more than the fulfillment of a justice-satisfying sacrifice. Of course, if we know our Bibles, we will want to affirm both of these things. The cross is about love and justice, which is why Dort is wise to begin Article 1 by affirming that "God is not only supremely merciful, but also supremely just." We never want to downplay the love of God at the cross. And yet we can't understand what love is at the cross unless we recognize that God sent his Son, in love, to be the wrath-satisfying propitiation for our sins (1 John 4:10).

We deserve punishment—temporal and eternal, in body and in soul (Article 1). The only way to escape this punishment is for God's wrath to be assuaged and his justice satisfied, which means our only hope is God's only begotten Son, "who was made to be sin and a curse for us, in our place" (Article 2). Everyone's prob-lem is sin, and the only remedy is Christ's sacrificial death on the cross. In my place condemned he stood, sealed my pardon with his blood. Hallelujah, what a Savior![1]

Infinity and Beyond (Articles 3–4)

Article 3: The Infinite Value of Christ's Death

The death of God's Son is the only and entirely complete sac-rifice and satisfaction for sins; it is of infinite value and worth, more than sufficient to atone for the sins of the whole world.

---

1. From the hymn by Philip P. Bliss, "Hallelujah! What a Savior," 1875.

Article 4: Reasons for This Infinite Value

This death is of such great value and worth for the reason that the person who suffered it is—as was necessary to be our Savior—not only a true and perfectly holy human, but also the only begotten Son of God, of the same eternal and infinite essence with the Father and the Holy Spirit. Another reason is that this death was accomplished by the experience of God's wrath and curse, which we by our sins had fully deserved.

It is sometimes assumed that the doctrine of definite atonement originated during the Reformation era of the sixteenth and seventeenth centuries, but the idea can be traced through the patristic and medieval periods as well. Although the doctrine was not articulated as clearly as it would be in later centuries, we can find versions of definite atonement from Augustine (354–430) to a theologian named Gottschalk (808–878) to medieval schoolmen like Peter Lombard (1100–1160) and Thomas Aquinas (1225–1274).[2] Of particular importance is the classic distinction given by Lombard, who stipulated that Christ "offered himself on the altar of the cross" and did so "for all with regard to the sufficiency of the price, but only for the elect with regard to its efficacy."[3] Even though Lombard's view, taken as a whole, was most consistent with a Reformed view of the atonement, the sufficient/efficient distinction by itself was ambiguous enough to be affirmed by most parts of the church. The debate was about the relationship between the sufficiency of the price and the efficacy for the elect.

---

2. See Lee Gatiss, *For Us and For Our Salvation: "Limited Atonement" in the Bible, Doctrine, History, and Ministry* (London: Latimer Trust, 2012), 60–67.

3. Peter Lombard, *The Sentences*, Bk. 3, *On the Incarnation of the Word*, trans. Giulio Silano (Toronto: Pontifical Institute of Medieval Studies, 2008), 86 (3.20.5). Quoted by Gatiss, *For Us and For Our Salvation*, 66.

We'll get to that controversy when we come to Article 8. For now, Dort wants to make clear that there is nothing lacking in the sacrificial death Christ made for sinners. Christ's work on the cross is "of infinite value and worth, more than sufficient to atone for the sins of the whole world" (Article 3). Notice that Dort does not say that Christ's death *did* sufficiently atone for the sins of the whole world. Instead, Dort affirms that Christ's death was sufficiently worthy that it could have (if that had been God's intention).

Notice two other important points in Article 4. First, we see why the death of Christ was so valuable. Medieval theologians often debated whether Christ's death was valuable (yet finite), based on his human nature, or valuable (and infinite), based on his divine nature. Dort argues that his death was of infinite value based on both: not only because he is "a true and perfectly holy human," but also because he is "the only begotten Son of God."[4] We cannot take away one whit of value from the atonement without taking away glory from the one who died to procure it.

Second, Dort assumes a view of the atonement that in our day has been called "penal substitutionary atonement." That is to say, Christ paid the penalty we deserved as a sin-bearing sacrifice in our place. Further, Dort does not hesitate to describe this penalty—the one we deserved and the one Christ paid—as "God's wrath and curse." Dort does not say the Son of God was damned, or that he went to hell, or any such language that would suggest a rupture in the Trinity. But it does maintain in Articles 2 and 4 that Christ became a curse for us and experienced the wrath of God in order to satisfy divine justice.

---

4. See Lee Gatiss, "The Synod of Dort and Definite Atonement," in *From Heaven He Came and Sought Her: Definite Atonement in Historical, Biblical, Theological, and Pastoral Perspective*, ed. David Gibson and Jonathan Gibson (Wheaton, IL: Crossway, 2013), 150.

Making Sense of Responsibility (Articles 5–7)

Article 5: The Mandate to Proclaim the Gospel to All

Moreover, it is the promise of the gospel that whoever believes in Christ crucified shall not perish but have eternal life. This promise, together with the command to repent and believe, ought to be announced and declared without differentiation or discrimination to all nations and people, to whom God in his good pleasure sends the gospel.

Article 6: Unbelief, a Human Responsibility

However, that many who have been called through the gospel do not repent or believe in Christ but perish in unbelief is not because the sacrifice of Christ offered on the cross is deficient or insufficient, but because they themselves are at fault.

Article 7: Faith God's Gift

But all who genuinely believe and are delivered and saved by Christ's death from their sins and from destruction receive this favor solely from God's grace—which God owes to no one—given to them in Christ from eternity.

✳ ✳ ✳

Whenever Christians champion a high view of God's sovereignty, there quickly follow questions about human responsibility. So before arguing that Christ died effectually only for the elect (Article 8), Dort clarifies what this means (and doesn't mean) in three different categories: evangelism, unbelief, and faith.

It's unfortunate that many people believe Reformed theology encourages indifference to the missionary task of the church, for here in the Canons of Dort—considered one of the high points of Calvinist confessional orthodoxy—we have a bold statement on the unequivocal mandate to preach the gospel to all nations. "This promise, together with the command to repent and believe, ought to be announced and declared without differentiation or discrimination to all nations and people" (Article 5).

Notice that Dort doesn't try to ground the Great Commission in the sufficiency of Christ's death (hence, Article 5 begins with "Moreover" instead of "Therefore"). A universal atonement is not required for universal gospel proclamation. Dort simply affirms what the Bible makes plain, that the gospel ought to be faithfully preached and freely offered to all peoples everywhere (Matt. 28:18–20; Acts 1:8).

Articles 6 and 7 emphasize the asymmetrical nature of faith and unbelief, the latter being entirely our fault (Article 6) and the former being a "favor solely from God's grace" (Article 7). Again, Dort is reminding us that the story of predestination, definite atonement, regeneration, and final glorification is the story of God's grace from start to finish. Left to ourselves, through no fault of Christ or the cross, we would choose wickedness and unbelief. Only by God's unmerited favor are we given the gift of election (in eternity) and the gift of saving faith (in time).

A Purposefully Definite Atonement (Article 8)

Article 8: *The Saving Effectiveness of Christ's Death*

For it was the entirely free plan and very gracious will and intention of God the Father that the enlivening and saving effectiveness of his Son's costly death should work itself out in all the elect, in order that God might grant justifying faith to them only and thereby lead them without fail to salvation. In other words, it was God's will that Christ through the blood of the cross (by which he confirmed the new covenant) should effectively redeem from every people, tribe, nation, and language all those and only those who were chosen from eternity to salvation and given to him by the Father; that Christ should grant them faith (which, like the Holy Spirit's other saving gifts, he acquired for them by his death). It was also God's will that Christ should cleanse them by his blood from all their sins, both original and actual, whether committed before or after their coming to faith; that he should faithfully preserve them to the very end; and that he should finally present them to himself, a glorious people, without spot or wrinkle.

We now come to the complicated and controversial part of this second main doctrine. For some later Reformed theologians, limited atonement was an inevitable conclusion once you've established that some people are eternally lost and that the atonement was a penal substitution. That is to say, if the atonement is a vicarious sacrifice whereby Christ died in the place of sinners such that the claims of divine justice against them have been satisfied, how can the atonement be anything but particular or definite? If some people do not believe, and if those unbelieving sinners are still under the wrath of God, it must not be that Christ died effectively for the sins of all, or else why would they be punished for their sins?

And yet, to be fair, this "double payment" argument is not Dort's stated logic (though many of the delegates would have affirmed it). We need to back up and try to understand the Arminian position first. Once we know what they were arguing for, it will be easier to see what Dort was arguing against.

In December 1618, the Remonstrants presented their *Opinions* before the Synod of Dort. Look at the first three points they make on "the universality of the merit of the death of Christ" (*Opinions* B.1, 2, 3). I'll put the Arminian points in *italics* and then provide my commentary in regular type.

1. *The price of the redemption which Christ offered to God the Father is not only in itself and by itself sufficient for the redemption of the whole human race but has also been paid for all men and for every man, according to the decree, will, and grace of God the Father; therefore no one is absolutely excluded from participation in the fruits of Christ's death by an absolute and antecedent decree of God.* While the Arminians talk about the sufficiency of Christ's death (like Dort ends up doing), they go one step farther and argue that redemption "has been paid for all men and for every man." The language of decree and will is also important, suggesting that God intended Christ's sacrificial death to be for everyone.

2. *Christ has, by the merit of his death, so reconciled God the Father to the whole human race that the Father, on account of that merit, without giving up his righteousness and truth, has been able and has willed to make and confirm a new covenant of grace with sinners and men liable to damnation.* The atonement was for every person, and so every person has been reconciled to God. But only in a certain sense. This is key: in the Arminian scheme, the death of Christ does not make man saved; it makes him saveable. Christ's sacrifice on the cross removed a barrier between God and man such that God is now able to enter into a new covenant with sinners.

3. *Though Christ has merited reconciliation with God and remission of sins for all men and for every man, yet no one, according to the pact of the new and gracious covenant, becomes a true partaker of the benefits obtained by the death of Christ in any other way than by faith; nor are sins forgiven to sinning men before they actually and truly believe in Christ.* Now we see the Arminian plan of

salvation more clearly. While Christ has merited forgiveness for every person, those benefits are not applied except by faith. Sinners are therefore reconciled to God (in that nothing can prevent the sinner from receiving God's grace), and yet the sinner is still liable to judgment unless the conditions of this new covenant are met. When the Remonstrants affirmed "Christ died for sinners," they did not mean "Christ died vicariously and efficaciously in the place of sinners." They meant, "Christ died so that sinners could come to him."

With all of this as background, let's look more closely at Dort's argument in Article 8. The two key words are *intention* and *effectively*. At issue were these two questions: "What outcome did God purpose to achieve by the cross?" And, "What did the death of Christ actually accomplish on the cross?"

To the first question, Dort said, "It was the entirely free plan and very gracious will and intention of God the Father that the enlivening and saving effectiveness of his Son's costly death should work itself out in all the elect, in order that God might grant justifying faith to them only and thereby lead them without fail to salvation." The issue was not whether Christ's death was sufficiently capable of saving all men, but whether God's *intention* was to put forth Christ as an effectual atoning sacrifice for every person. As we've seen already, the "sufficient for all, efficient for the elect" distinction had been around since Peter Lombard, but the formula had become a wax nose too malleable to be clarifying. Arminians acknowledged that the atonement was efficient only in the elect. But why? Dort maintained that the decisive factor in making the death of Christ efficacious for only some was not the human will, but God's will. The Remonstrants may have agreed on the outcome—an atoning sacrifice for the elect—but they denied a particular and divinely ordained intention in Christ's death. The issue could not be clarified by sufficiency and efficiency, but by sufficiency and intentionality.

The second crucial question is about the death of Christ and what it actually accomplished. Here the key word is *effectively*. "It was God's will that Christ through the blood of the cross (by which he confirmed the new covenant) should effectively redeem from every people, tribe, nation, and language all those and only those who were chosen from eternity to salvation and given to him by the Father." I said earlier that the debate at Dort was as much about the nature of the atonement as its extent. Both sides actually taught a "limited" atonement. While the Reformed famously limited the extent of the atonement, the Arminians limited the nature of the atonement. Christ's death became the means of removing original sin and granting men the prevenient grace necessary to believe (Rejection V). And yet there was no guarantee—not by human experience, let alone by divine decree—that anyone would enjoy the redeeming power of the cross. In order to defend the notion that Christ died for "all men and for every man," the Remonstrants championed an atonement that allowed for the potential salvation of everyone but actually secured the salvation of none.

Once again, the Rejection of Errors shines more light on the issues at stake. Dort stands opposed to those who teach that "God the Father appointed his Son to death on the cross without a fixed and definite plan to save anyone by name" (Rejection I), and that Christ's death did not establish a new covenant of grace (Heb. 7:22; 9:15) but only acquired the Father's right to enter into a new covenant with humanity (Rejection II). Dort saw in these doctrinal deviations not just a misplaced emphasis here or there, but the haunting specter of Pelagianism (Rejection III, VI). If "some rather than others come to share in the forgiveness of sins and eternal life depends on their own free choice," does this not suggest that

Christ died so that we can apply grace to ourselves by our own free choice (Rejection VI)? And if the grace of the cross depends on my free will to actualize it, hasn't salvation become a work instead of a gift? To be fair, that's not how the Arminians saw it, but Dort argued that it was the logic of their position.

Further Clarification and Complexities

Before turning to the final article, we need to address two other issues.

The first issue is what to do about the scriptural language of God loving the world (John 3:16) or Jesus being the propitiation for the sins of the whole world (1 John 2:2). This is the main exegetical reason for rejecting definite atonement. Maybe it makes logical sense in the Calvinist system, the argument goes, but the Bible clearly teaches that Christ died for the sins of the world.

That's true—Christ is the Lamb of God who takes away the sin of the world (John 1:29)—but what is meant by "the world"? The word *kosmos* (world) is used 186 times in the New Testament, seventy-seven times in the Gospel of John, twenty-three times in 1 John, and once in 2 John. There are three general meanings.

- *kosmos* can mean the world as the sum of all created things, the universe (e.g., "all things were made through him" [John 1:3]).

- *kosmos* can mean the world as the dwelling place of man, earth (e.g., "light has come into the world" [John 3:19]; "as he is so also we are in this world" [1 John 4:17]).

- *kosmos* can mean the world as the dwelling place of sin and sinners, fallen creation. And here there are two related meanings under this one heading. It can refer to fallen creation in subjection to the evil one (e.g., ruler of this world [John 12:31; 14:30; 16:11]; the whole world is under his control [1 John 5:19]; he is the one who is in the world [1 John 4:4]; chosen out of the world [John 17:6]; the world will hate us [1 John 3:13]). It can also refer to fallen creation as the object of God's love (e.g., God so loved the world [John 3:16]; God sent his Son into the world that we might live through him [4:9, 14]; he is the propitiation for the sins of the whole world [2:2]).

In summary, *kosmos* cannot be used to support an unlimited atonement. Most often, *world* refers to badness instead of bigness, and when it refers to bigness, *world* means everyone without distinction, not everyone without exception. So when 1 John 2:2 says Christ is the propitiation for the sins "of the whole world" (*holou tou kosmou*), it's a reference to all parts or all regions or all peoples of the world. The phrase is not used in Scripture to mean every person on the planet, which is why Paul can say to the Romans, "Your faith is proclaimed in all the world" (Rom. 1:8) when every individual on the planet did not know their faith, and Luke can tell us that "a decree went out from Caesar Augustus that all the world should be registered" (Luke 2:1) when the decree only covered the Roman Empire. *World* can mean people everywhere or all kinds of people, but it does not mean every person everywhere.

The second issue worth mentioning is the reality of some theological diversity at Dort.[5] When Martin Martinius of Bremen expressed his views on election rather awkwardly, Francis Gomarus was so upset that he challenged Martinius to a duel. The presiding officer tried to calm things with a time of prayer, but after the season of prayer Gomarus reissued his demand for a duel. Thankfully, the two did not fight to the death, but they did continue to spar verbally in debate.

More consequential, and more germane to limited atonement, was the disagreement from John Davenant of the British

---

5. For more on diversity at Dort, and on hypothetical universalism in particular, see Gatiss, "Synod of Dort and Definite Atonement," 154–60; Gatiss, *For Us and For Our Salvation*, 75–99.

delegation.[6] Davenant was determined to find a middle ground that the Lutheran church could accept and that would not be out of step with Anglican confessional documents as he read them. Davenant's view has come to be known as hypothetical universalism. When you hear "universalism," don't think "everyone is saved and no one goes to hell." That's not what universalism means in this context. Universal here is a reference to the extent of the atonement. Likewise, "hypothetical" in this sense doesn't mean "not real" but "conditional." Davenant agreed that God willed for Christ to die efficaciously only for the elect. In addition, however, he believed Christ *also* intended to die for all, with the salvific accomplishment of that death conditionally applied.

In other words, Davenant believed in a definite atonement for the elect and an indefinite atonement for all people based on the condition that they believe. This may sound like an amalgamation of Calvinism and Arminianism, but Davenant was clearly not an Arminian. He believed that the atonement effectively saved specific persons as willed by God's decree. This was the main thrust of Dort's doctrine.[7] At the same time, however, Davenant believed that God also decreed a universal, but also conditional, redemption for all people that proved, by God's design, to be hypothetical because only the elect enjoyed the saving benefits of the atonement.[8] While Dort never gives the least indication of supporting Davenant's view, contemporary proponents of hypothetical universalism point out that nothing in Dort explicitly forbids the view

---

6. For a scholarly and largely sympathetic view toward Davenant see Jonathan D. Moore, *English Hypothetical Universalism: John Preston and the Softening of Reformed Theology* (Grand Rapids, MI: Eerdmans, 2007), 187–213.

7. As Gatiss puts it, "What he and other Calvinistic hypothetical universalists held to were in fact variants of limited atonement, because they did see a definite, limited atonement toward the elect. They added a conditional intent on top of this or prior to this (not instead of this, as Arminians do)." *For Us and For our Salvation*, 99.

8. It should be noted that Davenant believed the nonelect did accrue nonsaving benefits from the atonement (e.g., a sense of sin and a fear of punishment), though this was not a position taken up by Dort.

either. Personally, I find the view speculative, lacking in scriptural support, and, with its completely ineffectual universal atonement, hardly a "softer" or more palatable form of Calvinism.[9]

A Gloriously Effectual Atonement (Article 9)

Article 9: The Fulfillment of God's Plan

This plan, arising out of God's eternal love for the elect, from the beginning of the world to the present time has been powerfully carried out and will also be carried out in the future, the gates of hell seeking vainly to prevail against it. As a result, the elect are gathered into one, all in their own time, and there is always a church of believers founded on Christ's blood, a church which steadfastly loves, persistently worships, and here and in all eternity praises him as her Savior who laid down his life for her on the cross, as a bridegroom for his bride.

As we saw at the beginning of this chapter, the doctrine of definite atonement is meant for doxology. We rejoice, not because the extent of the atonement is limited, but because the nature of the atonement is not. The Arminians believed that the cross brought people into reconciliation with God and made salvation now available for all, but the atonement itself did not insure any

---

9. Following Dort, for much of the seventeenth century, the international Reformed community was divided over the views of Moise Amyraut, a professor at Saumur, France, who also posited a version of hypothetical universalism. Unlike Davenant's version, however, Amyraut altered the order of the decrees. This may seem like splitting hairs, but it's important to note that in Davenant's view the conditional decree stood alongside the unconditional one. God willed to effectively redeem the elect while at the same time willing to redeem all people who believe. By contrast, Amyraut argued that God first decreed a universal atonement (according to his revealed will), but then, upon realizing that none would be saved by that decree alone, he decreed (according to this secret will) that a group of sinners would be enabled to believe. Amyraut's theology was put outside confessional Reformed boundaries by the (short-lived) Formula Consensus Helvetica (1675). Four-point Calvinists are sometimes labeled Amryaldians, so-called because of their dependence, intentional or unintentional, upon Amyraut. See Amar Djaballah, "Controversy on Universal Grace," and Donald Macleod, "Definite Atonement and the Divine Decree," in *From Heaven He Came*, 165–99; 401–36.

saving efficacy. Dort, on the other hand, teaches that the application of redemption cannot be separated from the accomplishment of the atonement. The atonement describes what God intended and what Christ actually achieved.

The point of this definite atonement is not to truncate the mercy of God, but to celebrate the triumph that Christ died effectively and savingly but for his particular people. The Good Shepherd lays his life down, not for the goats, but for the sheep (John 10:11). This is why John 6 says Jesus came to save those the Father had given to him, and why Matthew 1:21 says he died for his people, John 15:13 says he died for his friends, Acts 20:28 says he died for the church, and Ephesians 5:25 says he died for his bride.

The doctrine of particular redemption is worth defining and defending because it gets to the heart of the gospel. Did Christ's work on the cross make it possible for sinners to come to God? Or did Christ's work on the cross efficaciously reconcile sinners to God? Does the death of Christ make all people saveable or make his people saved?

We cannot pull at the thread of particular redemption without the whole ball of Reformed soteriology coming loose. All five points are related as God wills the plan of salvation from election in eternity, to definite atonement in first-century Judea, to irresistible grace at a specific moment in your life, to the perseverance of the saints unto the end of the age and into the age to come. What God decrees will come to pass, and everything we enjoy in Christ is rooted in his divine decree. All the gifts of salvation are absolutely decreed by the Father, definitely purchased by the Son, and infallibly applied by the Holy Spirit.

To the praise of his glory.

3

Human Corruption, Divine Conversion

The Third and Fourth Main Points of Doctrine

Imagine two different scenarios and two different gifts.

In scenario one, your father comes home from work on your sixteenth birthday and announces he has a surprise for you. He takes you to the local car dealership and points to a brand-new, sporty convertible. He tells you the car is yours if you want it. He's paid for it and signed all the papers. All you have to do is grab the keys, hop in the car, and drive your shiny new vehicle off the lot. That's quite a gift: a pricey convertible for free, if you decide you want it.

Here's another scenario. You are lying unconscious on a hospital bed. You don't know where you are, who you are, or what is going on. You should be dead. In fact, the doctor pronounced you dead a minute ago, but now your heart is beating. The hospital staff had pumped blood into your veins when you had bled out from a massive laceration on your leg. That's quite a gift: someone else's blood for free, put into you when you had no ability to ask for it, resist it, or receive it.

No analogy is perfect, so don't read spiritual significance into every detail. Don't focus on the value of the gift (Arminians believe that God gives new life, not new cars) or whether the recipient is dead or alive (though that's important on another level). Think instead about the nature of the gifts. Both are freely given. Both are undeserved. But one gift is presented for you to accept, while the other gift is a new quality infused within us. The gift, as represented in these scenarios, is not salvation, per se, but faith. Is saving faith a gift that we can accept or deny, or is it a new principle worked in us by God's sovereign and unfailingly effectual will? That question is at the heart of Dort's Third and Fourth Main Points of Doctrine.

Since Dort combines corruption and conversion in one section, putting the third and fourth points together, I'll do the same. Two sections for the price of one! I'll move through each article, noting one or two key ideas with each article along the way.

What a Fall It Was (Articles 1–3)

Article 1: The Effect of the Fall on Human Nature

Human beings were originally created in the image of God and were furnished in mind with a true and sound knowledge of the Creator and things spiritual, in will and heart with righteousness, and in all emotions with purity; indeed, the whole human being was holy. However, rebelling against God at the devil's instigation and by their own free will, they deprived themselves of these outstanding gifts. Rather, in their place they brought upon themselves blindness, terrible darkness, futility, and distortion of judgment in their minds; perversity, defiance, and hardness in their hearts and wills; and finally impurity in all their emotions.

Article 2: The Spread of Corruption

Human beings brought forth children of the same nature as themselves after the fall. That is to say, being corrupt they brought forth corrupt children. The corruption spread, by God's just judgment, from Adam and Eve to all their descendants—except for Christ alone—not by way of imitation (as in former times the Pelagians would have it) but by way of the propagation of their perverted nature.

Article 3: Total Inability

Therefore, all people are conceived in sin and are born children of wrath, unfit for any saving good, inclined to evil, dead in their sins, and slaves to sin. Without the grace of the regenerating Holy Spirit they are neither willing nor able to return to God, to reform their distorted nature, or even to dispose themselves to such reform.

Article 1 describes the state of man before and after the fall. "Human beings were originally created in the image of God," holy and pure in mind, will, heart, and emotions.[1] This all changed after Adam and Eve rebelled against God by "their own free will." We often think of free will as being the opposite, in some sense, of God's sovereignty. But strictly speaking, the freedom of the will has to do with whether the will is in bondage to sin. Prior to the fall, human beings had free will (in this sense), but now our wills, apart from regeneration, are bound to sin. What was holy and pure has become dark, futile, and distorted. Every part of us— mind, will, heart, and emotions—has been corrupted by the fall.

---

1. Older translations of Dort have "affection" instead of "emotion," which is a less common word to us but technically more precise. Affections were understood as inclinations and dispositions, not emotional states that passively rush over us.

This corruption has spread from Adam and Eve to the whole human race. There's an important distinction along these lines in Article 2. We have all become polluted, Dort says, not by following the bad example of Adam and Eve or by imitating our sinful parents, "but by the way of the propagation of their perverted nature." We don't just sin; we are sinners. Sin is not just something we do when we follow bad examples; it's who we are in our very nature.

The result is that we come into the world with an inherited guilt (i.e., children of wrath) and an inherited depravity (Rom. 5:12, 16; 6:23). We are conceived in sin, dead in sin, and slaves to sin. The heart is deceitful above all things (Jer. 17:9). We are children of disobedience (Eph. 2:3) and inclined to evil all the time (Gen. 6:5). The conclusion Dort reaches from all this is as important as it is correct: as spiritually dead men, women, and children, we are totally unable to return to God or reform our nature (Article 3). This means we need more than divine assistance or cooperating grace to be saved. We need a sovereignly administered resurrection from the dead.

Not Enough (Articles 4–5)

Article 4: The Inadequacy of the Light of Nature

There is, to be sure, a certain light of nature remaining in all people after the fall, by virtue of which they retain some notions about God, natural things, and the difference between what is moral and immoral, and demonstrate a certain eagerness for virtue and for good outward behavior. But this light of nature is far from enabling humans to come to a saving knowledge of God and conversion to him—so far, in fact, that they do not use it rightly even in matters of nature and society. Instead, in various ways they completely distort this light, whatever its precise character, and suppress it in unrighteousness. In doing so all people render themselves without excuse before God.

Article 5: The Inadequacy of the Law

In this respect, what is true of the light of nature is true also of the Ten Commandments given by God through Moses specifically to the Jews. For humans cannot obtain saving grace through the Decalogue, because, although it does expose the magnitude of their sin and increasingly convict them of their guilt, yet it does not offer a remedy or enable them to escape from human misery, and, indeed, weakened as it is by the flesh, leaves the offender under the curse.

The doctrine of total depravity is sometimes misunderstood to mean that people are as bad as they can possibly be. But the "total" is with respect to the *extent* of the depravity (mind, will, heart, emotions), not to the degree. Some Arminians thought that depravity had affected primarily the mind but not the will. Further, some believed that God would not condemn people for original sin, but only for failing to believe in Christ after being given prevenient grace. Dort, by contrast, taught original sin, original guilt, and total inability.

This is not to say that the divine fingerprints have been completely scrubbed from God's image bearers. Even after the fall, we still have "a certain light of nature," "some notions about God," an awareness of right and wrong, and an eagerness for "good outward behavior" (Article 4). Dort affirms "common grace."[2] What is denied is that this common grace is sufficient or effective for revealing Christ, for faith, and for repentance (Rejection V).

This is the point of Romans 1. God's eternal power and divine nature can be clearly seen in creation, but we have suppressed this knowledge and exchanged the truth about God for

---

2. "Common grace" is the phrase used in the Rejection of Errors. More recent notions of common grace (from Abraham Kuyper and his followers) should not automatically be read into Dort's language. Dort uses the phrase as a synonym for "light of nature."

a lie (Rom. 1:18–25). General revelation is not enough to save us. Neither is the law of God a sufficient "remedy" for sin and "human misery" (Article 5). We need more than the splendor of creation and the sanctity of the Ten Commandments. An external testimony will not do. We must be made new from the inside out.

The Gospel Call (Articles 6–9)

Article 6: The Saving Power of the Gospel

What, therefore, neither the light of nature nor the law can do, God accomplishes by the power of the Holy Spirit, through the Word or the ministry of reconciliation. This is the gospel about the Messiah, through which it has pleased God to save believers, in both the Old and the New Testaments.

Article 7: God's Freedom in Revealing the Gospel

In the Old Testament, God revealed this secret of his will to a small number; in the New Testament (now without any distinction between peoples) God discloses it to a large number. The reason for this difference must not be ascribed to the greater worth of one nation over another, or to a better use of the light of nature, but to the free good pleasure and undeserved love of God. Therefore, those who receive so much grace, beyond and in spite of all they deserve, ought to acknowledge it with humble and thankful hearts. On the other hand, with the apostle they ought to adore (but certainly not inquisitively search into) the severity and justice of God's judgments on the others, who do not receive this grace.

Article 8: The Earnest Call of the Gospel

Nevertheless, all who are called through the gospel are called earnestly. For urgently and most genuinely God makes known in the Word what is pleasing to him: that those who are called should come to God. God also earnestly promises rest for their souls and eternal life to all who do come and believe.

Article 9: Human Responsibility for Rejecting the Gospel

The fact that many who are called through the ministry of the gospel do not come and are not brought to conversion must not be blamed on the gospel, nor on Christ, who is offered through the gospel, nor on God, who calls them through the gospel and even bestows various gifts on them, but on the people themselves who are called. Some in self-assurance do not even entertain the Word of life; others do entertain it but do not take it to heart, and for that reason, after the fleeting joy of a temporary faith, they relapse; others choke the seed of the Word with the thorns of life's cares and with the pleasures of the world and bring forth no fruits. This our Savior teaches in the parable of the sower (Matt. 13).

※ ※ ※

What the light of nature and the law cannot do, the preaching of the gospel is able to accomplish (Article 6). In both the Old and the New Testaments, God has saved people in the same way: through the hope of the Messiah and the ministry of reconciliation. The gospel is "the power of God for salvation to everyone who believes, to the Jew first and also to the Greek" (Rom. 1:16).

Every Christian understands that people are saved through the call of the gospel. What Dort makes clear is that there is both a general earnest call and a saving effectual call, and that one does not contradict the other. The Arminians rejected the notion that God could call people according to his revealed will whom he did not also call according to his secret will (see *Opinions* C.9). By contrast, Dort believes that all people can be "genuinely" called by the gospel (Article 16). The promise of eternal life for all who repent of their sins and believe in Christ is a sincere, unbreakable promise. While we do not preach indiscriminately "Jesus died for you" (we see no such gospel announcement in the New Testament), we can confidently proclaim to all that Jesus died to take away the sin of the world (John 1:29) and that "everyone who calls on the name of the Lord will be saved" (Rom. 10:13).

If the general call is earnestly for all, and the saving effectual call only for some, what should we conclude about those who believe and those who do not? According to Dort, we must not conclude the same thing. Human beings are always responsible for rejecting the saving message of Christ. The failure to be converted "must not be blamed on the gospel, nor on Christ, . . . nor on God" (Article 9). God does not prevent anyone from coming to him (John 6:37). He never turns away the humble sinner with the words, "Sorry, you were not elect." Men and women reject the gospel not because God makes them, but because men and women are by nature children of disobedience.

If rejecting the gospel call is entirely our fault, we must be equally clear that embracing the gospel call is entirely due to God's "free good pleasure" and his undeserved love (Article 7). If we respond to the preaching of the Word with faith and repentance, it is not because of our superior heart or will, but "in spite of all [we] deserve." That we were given grace to believe is a reason for "humble and thankful hearts," not a reason to "inquisitively search into" the sovereign will of God (Article 7).

Regeneration and the Gift of Faith (Articles 10–14)

Article 10: Conversion as the Work of God

The fact that others who are called through the ministry of the gospel do come and are brought to conversion must not be credited to human effort, as though one distinguishes oneself by free choice from others who are furnished with equal or sufficient grace for faith and conversion (as the proud heresy of Pelagius maintains). No, it must be credited to God: just as from eternity God chose his own in Christ, so within time God effectively calls them, grants them faith and repentance, and, having rescued them from the dominion of darkness, brings them into the kingdom of his Son, in order that they may declare the wonderful deeds of the One who called them out of darkness into this marvelous light, and may boast not in themselves, but in the Lord, as apostolic words frequently testify in Scripture.

Article 11: The Holy Spirit's Work in Conversion

Moreover, when God carries out this good pleasure in the elect, or works true conversion in them, God not only sees to it that the gospel is proclaimed to them outwardly, and enlightens their minds powerfully by the Holy Spirit so that they may rightly understand and discern the things of the Spirit of God, but, by the effective operation of the same regenerating Spirit, God also penetrates into the inmost being, opens the closed heart, softens the hard heart, and circumcises the heart that is uncircumcised. God infuses new qualities into the will, making the dead will alive, the evil one good, the unwilling one willing, and the stubborn one compliant. God activates and strengthens the will so that, like a good tree, it may be enabled to produce the fruits of good deeds.

Article 12: Regeneration a Supernatural Work

And this is the regeneration, the new creation, the raising from the dead, and the making alive so clearly proclaimed in the Scriptures, which God works in us without our help. But this certainly does not happen only by outward teaching, by moral persuasion, or by such a way of working that, after God's work is done, it remains in human power whether or not to be reborn or converted. Rather, it is an entirely supernatural work, one that is at the same time most powerful and most pleasing, a marvelous, hidden, and inexpressible work, which is not less than or inferior in power to that of creation or of raising the dead, as Scripture (inspired by the author of this work) teaches. As a result, all those in whose hearts God works in this marvelous way are certainly, unfailingly, and effectively reborn and do actually believe. And then the will, now renewed, is not only activated and motivated by God, but in being activated by God is also itself active. For this reason, people themselves, by that grace which they have received, are also rightly said to believe and to repent.

Article 13: The Incomprehensible Way of Regeneration

In this life believers cannot fully understand the way this work occurs; meanwhile, they rest content with knowing and experiencing that, by this grace of God, they do believe with the heart and love their Savior.

Article 14: The Way God Gives Faith

In this way, therefore, faith is a gift of God, not in the sense that it is offered by God for people to choose, but that it is in actual fact bestowed on them, breathed and infused into them. Nor is it a gift in the sense that God bestows only the potential to believe, but then awaits assent—the act of believing—by human choice; rather, it is a gift in the sense that God who works both willing and acting and, indeed, works all things in all people and produces in them both the will to believe and the belief itself.

❄ ❄ ❄

In this section we come to the heart of the controversy regarding human corruption and divine conversion. The most important distinctions between Arminian theology and Reformed theology (on this particular subject) come through in these articles. So let's work our way through the key points in each article.

Article 10 reinforces several points we've seen before: that conversion must "not be credited to human effort," that conversion is God's work, and that they who believe "may boast not in themselves." We also see how Dort's doctrinal emphases are interconnected. Just as God, from eternity, "chose his own in Christ, so within time God effectively calls them." Whereas Arminianism is shot through with conditionalism—a conditional election based on foreseen faith, a conditional application of the atonement based on the exercise of faith, and a conditional conversion based on human willing and receiving—so Reformed soteriology is unconditional through and through. In eternity, God freely chose us; on Calvary, he definitely redeemed us; and in time, he effectively converts us. Either divine sovereignty or human decision must be the decisive factor from start to finish.

We get a clearer picture of this sovereign work of God in Article 11. It would be unfair to say that the Arminians did not believe in human depravity and divine grace. Like the Calvinists at Dort, the Arminians taught that men and women need the Spirit's work in their lives in order to exercise faith and repentance. The difference lies in how both sides understood the Spirit's work in conversion. The Arminians maintained that all people have been given sufficient grace for faith and conversion. Faith is a gift offered not to all, but unilaterally infused in none.

By contrast, Dort says we are in need of more than enlightening or enabling grace. God doesn't effect conversion by mere "moral persuasion" (Rejection VII). Rather, he "penetrates into the inmost being, opens the closed heart, softens the hard heart, and circumcises the heart that is uncircumcised." In other words, God "infuses new qualities into the will, making the dead will alive, the evil one good, the unwilling one willing, and the stubborn one compliant." We believe because God unilaterally changes the human heart so that we can *and will* believe.

This point is further expounded in Article 12. When the Arminians defended their view of conversion at Dort, they highlighted our need for divine grace, but they called it a "preceding or prevenient, awakening, following and cooperating grace" (*Opinions* C.2). As much as I love Wesley's hymn "And Can It Be," when he wrote, as an Arminian, about how "thine eye diffused a quickening ray" and how "my chains fell off, my heart was free, I rose, went forth, and followed Thee," he was talking about the prevenient awakening grace of God that enables the human will to make a decision for Christ. This is, to quote the Arminians at Dort, the "sufficient grace for faith and conversion" that falls not only to the lot of those who will believe "but also of those who are not actually converted" (*Opinions* C.6). This is why the Arminians denied "irresistible" grace. "Man is able of himself," they maintained, "to despise that grace and not to believe" (*Opinions* C.5).

With this background, we can see how different is a Reformed understanding of grace. For Dort, regeneration is "an entirely supernatural work," one in which God "works in us without our help" (Article 12). One of the hallmarks of Reformed soteriology is the biblical conviction that regeneration precedes faith. That is, if we are to believe in Christ, God must work in our hearts so that we are "certainly, unfailingly, and effectively reborn" (Article 12). In the miracle of regeneration, we bring nothing and do nothing. The work is not synergistic (two working together) but entirely and utterly monergistic (according to the power of only one working). If we are actually dead in our sins and trespasses, not merely sick and struggling, how could regeneration be anything other than a work of sovereign, supernatural, unilateral, irresistible grace? As Dort puts it, this "inexpressible work" is "not less than or inferior in power to that of creation or of raising the dead" (Article 12). Do you want to see miracles? Go to church on Sunday. All around you will be walking miracles—men and women who were dead and are now alive.

What then can we do to be regenerated? By Dort's logic, that is the wrong question. We "cannot fully understand the way this work occurs" (Article 13). We cannot make ourselves be born again, just as we cannot make ourselves be born (John 1:12–13). We do not work for the miracle of regeneration. That would be a contradiction in terms. Our part is to "rest content with knowing and experiencing" the new birth, being assured that if we "believe with the heart and love the Savior" we have been regenerated (Article 13). "The wind blows where it wishes, and you hear its sound, but you do not know where it comes from or where it goes. So it is with everyone who is born of the Spirit" (John 3:8).

This leads to one last clarifying, and crucial, point in Article 14. While we must exercise faith as an act of the will, faith "is a gift of God, not in the sense that it is offered by God for people to choose, but that it is in actual fact bestowed on them, breathed and infused into them." This brings us back to the two scenarios at the opening of the chapter. Faith, according to Dort, is not like the car we have to drive off the lot but like the blood transfusion poured into our veins when we were utterly helpless to help ourselves. In other words, faith is not something outside of us that we grab hold of. It is a work that God works in us, producing "both the will to believe and the belief itself."

Of Wills and Ways (Articles 15–17)

Article 15: Responses to God's Grace

God does not owe this grace to anyone. For what could God owe to those who have nothing to give that can be paid back? Indeed, what could God owe to those who have nothing of their own to give but sin and falsehood? Therefore those who receive this grace owe and give eternal thanks to God alone; those who do not receive it either do not care at all about these spiritual things and are satisfied with themselves in their condition, or else in self-assurance foolishly boast about having something which they lack. Furthermore, following the example of the apostles, we are to think and to speak in the most favorable way about those who outwardly profess their faith and better their lives, for the inner chambers of the heart are unknown to us. But for others who have not yet been called, we are to pray to the God who calls things that do not exist as though they did. In no way, however, are we to pride ourselves as better than they, as though we had distinguished ourselves from them.

Article 16: Regeneration's Effect

However, just as by the fall humans did not cease to be human, endowed with intellect and will, and just as sin, which has spread through the whole human race, did not abolish the nature of the human race but distorted and spiritually killed it, so also this divine grace of regeneration does not act in people as if they were blocks and stones; nor does it abolish the will and its properties or coerce a reluctant will by force, but spiritually revives, heals, reforms, and—in a manner at once pleasing and powerful—bends it back. As a result, a ready and sincere obedience of the Spirit now begins to prevail where before the rebellion and resistance of the flesh were completely dominant. In this the true and spiritual restoration and freedom of our will consists. Thus, if the marvelous Maker of every good thing were not dealing with us, we would have no hope of getting up from our fall by our own free choice, by which we plunged ourselves into ruin when still standing upright.

Article 17: God's Use of Means in Regeneration

Just as the almighty work by which God brings forth and sustains our natural life does not rule out but requires the use of means, by which God, according to his infinite wisdom and goodness, has wished to exercise that divine power, so also the aforementioned supernatural work by which God regenerates us in no way rules out or cancels the use of the gospel, which God in great wisdom has appointed to be the seed of regeneration and the food of the soul. For this reason, the apostles and the teachers who followed them taught the people in a godly manner about this grace of God, to give God the glory and to humble all pride, and yet did not neglect meanwhile to keep the people, by means of the holy admonitions of the gospel, under the administration of the Word, the sacraments, and discipline. So even today it is out of the question that the teachers or those taught in the church should presume to test God by separating what God in his good pleasure has wished to be closely joined together. For grace is bestowed through admonitions, and the more readily we perform our duty, the more lustrous the benefit of God working in us usually is, and the better that work advances. To God alone, both for the means and for their saving fruit and effectiveness, all glory is owed forever. Amen.

As we've seen before at the end of a Main Point of Doctrine, in these final articles Dort tries to clear up potential misunderstandings about a Reformed view of soteriology. Let's conclude, then, with three clarifying comments.

First, irresistible grace ought to produce in the believer humility and charity, not pride and suspicion. Just as God did not choose the elect because of anything in them, so he has not converted the destitute because they were in any way deserving. In no way are we who believe "to pride ourselves as better than they, as though we had distinguished ourselves from them" (Article 15). Likewise, we should not nitpick our fellow believers as if we need to pry open their spiritual innards and determine what God has really done in there. No, Dort says, "we are to think and to speak in the most favorable way about those who outwardly profess their faith and better their lives." Insisting upon regenerate church membership (which we ought to do) is not an excuse for acting the part of judge, jury, and executioner. We are simply looking for a credible profession of faith and the fruit of the Spirit.

Second, in regeneration the human will is renewed, not removed. People often criticize Reformed theology for reducing men and women to robots or puppets on a string. But Dort will not let us settle for such caricatures. Puppets have no will of their own. Their movements are manipulated by an external force. This is not what Calvinists believe (or not what they should believe!) about God's sovereignty. The "divine grace of regeneration does not act in people as if they were blocks and stones; nor does it abolish the will and its properties or coerce a reluctant will by force, but spiritually revives, heals, reforms, and—in a manner at once pleasing and powerful—bends it back" (Article 16).

This is massively important. Reformed people believe in making choices. We do not hesitate to call people to repent and believe. We believe in human willing and doing. We *also* believe that God must infuse the will with new properties if we are to will or do anything pleasing to him. That's why Dort is careful to describe faith as the gift God works in us by the renewal of the will. Irresistible grace is what God supernaturally accomplishes by the internal and effectual converting power of the Spirit, not what God forces upon us by external compulsion and coercion.

Think about peas (and I promise, I won't make you think about them for long). Most sane, high-functioning children do not like peas. The only way to get peas into a squirmy child is to forcibly hold the child still, pry open the lower jaw, and ram those green spheres of squirty-ness into the face. "You're going to eat every last one of those peas if I have to pin you to the floor. And you'll like it!" That is *not* what we mean by irresistible grace. God does not save us by forcing grace upon us against our will (or by obliterating the will). Instead, he renews, changes, and transforms our will. So—if you permit the analogy to get a bit strange—now that our will is infused with a new property, we can see and taste and touch and discern that the peas were actually jelly beans all along (I told you this was a miracle). God doesn't shove the vegetables of grace down our throats. He changes our wills so that now—according to the newness of our sovereignly transformed wills—we want to take in the sweet forgiveness he provides for us.

Third, God works the miracle of regeneration by way of means. Yes, God is sovereign. Yes, the Spirit blows where he wills. Yes, the Lord choses to have mercy on whom he will have mercy. But the Lord has also chosen to effect this regeneration by "the use of the gospel" (Article 17).

When I was in college I had a professor who argued that he was so Reformed that he believed people could be born again whether they had ever heard of Christ or not. Many students found his logic persuasive: if God is sovereign, then who's to say he can't regenerate in a thousand different ways? And yet Dort has no place for this kind of anonymous Christianity. God has willed to call his people and keep his people through the ordinary means of Word, sacrament, and discipline. "It is out of the question," Dort maintains, "that the teachers or those taught in the church should presume to test God by separating what God in his good pleasure has wished to be closely joined together" (Article 17). According to God's plan, "faith comes from hearing, and hearing through the word of Christ" (Rom. 10:17). What God has joined together, let no one separate.

4

He Who Began a Good Work Will Bring It to Completion

The Fifth Main Point of Doctrine

Of the so-called five points of Calvinism, this is the one most people want to affirm. And yet it's also the one many people misunderstand. A lot of Christians will gladly hold to the doctrine of "eternal security" or "once saved, always saved." And that's good—maybe. It all depends on what people mean by these slogans.

Too often, Christians have a mechanical view of salvation and, therefore, an unbiblical view of eternal security. They see "getting saved" as something that infallibly took place when you walked the aisle, raised your hand, prayed the sinner's prayer, or threw your pinecone into the fire at summer camp. And now that you've taken that step, well, "once saved, always saved." No matter what you do. No matter what you say. No matter how you live your life. As long as you took that magical step of salvation, you have your get-out-of-jail-free card forever, and God is obliged to redeem you on the last day.

That's not what the Bible teaches. Those who "believe in the name of the Son of God" already "have eternal life" (1 John 5:13). At the same time, those who do not "continue with us" demonstrate that they were "not of us" (1 John 2:19). Dort's doctrine is not about a spiritual trump card that negates all other evidences (or lack thereof). Just think of the two *P* words: *perseverance* and *preservation*. This is not a doctrine to encourage spiritual lethargy and moral laxity. This is a doctrine that encourages the Christian to actively *persevere* in faith, in repentance, and in godliness because we have confidence that God will unfailingly *preserve* the elect. This final point in Dort is all about what God works in us as we work out our salvation with fear and trembling (Phil. 2:12–13).

In the end, eternal security is wonderfully true, and, yes, once we are saved, we will always be saved. But we must move past the slogans to the sturdier doctrines underneath. Only by examining Dort's theological care and pastoral concern will we see how God's sustaining grace works and what good news it is that it does.

Realistic and Resolute (Articles 1–8)

Article 1: The Regenerate Not Entirely Free from Sin

Those people whom God according to his purpose calls into fellowship with his Son Jesus Christ our Lord and regenerates by the Holy Spirit, God also sets free from the dominion and slavery of sin, though not entirely from the flesh and from the body of sin as long as they are in this life.

Article 2: The Believer's Reaction to Sins of Weakness

Hence daily sins of weakness arise, and blemishes cling to even the best works of saints, giving them continual cause to

humble themselves before God, to flee for refuge to Christ crucified, to put the flesh to death more and more by the Spirit of
supplication and by holy exercises of godliness, and to strain
toward the goal of perfection, until they are freed from this
body of death and reign with the Lamb of God in heaven.

Article 3: God's Preservation of the Converted

Because of these remnants of sin dwelling in them and also
because of the temptations of the world and Satan, those who
have been converted could not remain standing in this grace
if left to their own resources. But God is faithful, mercifully
strengthening them in the grace once conferred on them and
powerfully preserving them in it to the end.

Article 4: The Danger of True Believers'
Falling into Serious Sins

The power of God strengthening and preserving true believers
in grace is more than a match for the flesh. Yet those converted
are not always so activated and motivated by God that in
certain specific actions they cannot by their own fault depart
from the leading of grace, be led astray by the desires of the
flesh, and give in to them. For this reason they must constantly
watch and pray that they may not be led into temptations.
When they fail to do this, not only can they be carried away
by the flesh, the world, and Satan into sins, even serious and
outrageous ones, but also by God's just permission they sometimes are so carried away—witness the sad cases, described in
Scripture, of David, Peter, and other saints falling into sins.

Article 5: The Effects of Such Serious Sins

By such monstrous sins, however, they greatly offend God,
deserve the sentence of death, grieve the Holy Spirit, suspend

the exercise of faith, severely wound the conscience, and some-times lose the awareness of grace for a time—until, after they have returned to the right way by genuine repentance, God's fatherly face again shines upon them.

Article 6: *God's Saving Intervention*

For God, who is rich in mercy, according to the unchangeable purpose of election does not take the Holy Spirit from his own completely, even when they fall grievously. Neither does God let them fall down so far that they forfeit the grace of adoption and the state of justification, or commit the sin which leads to death (the sin against the Holy Spirit), and plunge themselves, entirely forsaken by God, into eternal ruin.

Article 7: *Renewal to Repentance*

For, in the first place, God preserves in those saints when they fall the imperishable seed from which they have been born again, lest it perish or be dislodged. Secondly, by his Word and Spirit God certainly and effectively renews them to repentance so that they have a heartfelt and godly sorrow for the sins they have committed; seek and obtain, through faith and with a contrite heart, forgiveness in the blood of the Mediator; expe-rience again the grace of a reconciled God; through faith adore God's mercies; and from then on more eagerly work out their own salvation with fear and trembling.

Article 8: *The Certainty of This Preservation*

So it is not by their own merits or strength but by God's un-deserved mercy that they neither forfeit faith and grace totally nor remain in their downfalls to the end and are lost. With respect to themselves this not only easily could happen, but also undoubtedly would happen; but with respect to God it cannot possibly happen. God's plan cannot be changed; God's promise cannot fail; the calling according to God's purpose cannot be revoked; the merit of Christ as well as his interceding and preserving cannot be nullified; and the sealing of the Holy Spirit can neither be invalidated nor wiped out.

✳ ✳ ✳

These first eight articles can be summarized with two words: *realistic* and *resolute*. The picture Dort paints of the perseverance of the saints is one that is realistic about the human condition on this side of heaven, while at the same time confident in the resolute nature of God's commitment to his chosen ones.

Look at how realistic Dort is about the struggles that still beset redeemed people. Although God sets us free "from the dominion and slavery of sin," we are "not entirely [free] from the flesh and from the body of sin as long as [we] are in this life" (Article 1). We are still prone to "daily sins of weakness," and even our best works are marked by "blemishes" (Article 2). There is no human (except for Jesus) who never sins (Eccles. 7:20), and if we say we are without sin, we deceive ourselves and the truth is not in us (1 John 1:9).

What's more, Dort understands that sin continues to be offensive to God, even after we have been converted. Contrary to some muddleheaded piety, regeneration and justification do not make God blind to our faults, as if the cross makes post-conversion sins invisible. To the contrary, our "monstrous sins"—and Dort is talking about believers here—"greatly offend God, deserve the sentence of death, grieve the Holy Spirit, suspend the exercise of faith," and "severely wound the conscience." We can even "lose the awareness of grace for a time" when we are mired in such disobedience (Article 5).

The hymn writer was right: "Prone to wander, Lord I feel it; prone to leave the God I love." In fact, because of the continuing presence of indwelling sin and because of ongoing temptations from the world and Satan, left to ourselves, we would certainly not remain in God's grace (Article 3). Apart from God's intervention, it would not only be possible for men and women to forfeit saving faith; it "undoubtedly would happen" (Article 8).

But Dort isn't just realistic about our tendency to quit the race of faith; the canons are confident in God's resolute purposes to get us safely to the finish line. God will not take the Holy Spirit from his own; neither will he "let them fall down so far that they forfeit the grace of adoption and the state of justification" (Article 6). Although we sin and struggle and may even stray from the path, God's purpose in election will stand (Rom. 9:11). In the end, it is not possible to destroy and deceive the elect (Matt. 24:24; 1 Pet. 1:5). "The power of God strengthening and preserving true believers in grace is more than a match for the flesh" (Article 4). Or as John puts it, "he who is in you is greater than he who is in the world" (1 John 4:4).

But notice that this preserving grace is more than a passive protection. God causes us to persevere by actively working in what we need to keep walking with Christ. According to Article 7, this means two things. First, God does not let the seed of the Word die or be removed. That is to say, God keeps those sermons and those Bible studies and those memory verses doing their good work in our hearts. Second, he renews us unto repentance. True believers will always come back to a "heartfelt and godly sorrow for their sins." We will, then, "through faith and with a contrite heart" seek and obtain forgiveness in the blood of the Mediator. And, finally, we will "experience again the grace of a reconciled God."

Dort has no place for carnal Christianity, but it does allow and even expect there to be contrite Christians. The doctrine of perseverance does not negate repentance; it leads us to repentance. The grace that saves a wretch like me is also the grace that will lead me home.

Blessed Assurance (Articles 9–14)

Article 9: The Assurance of This Preservation

Concerning this preservation of those chosen to salvation and concerning the perseverance of true believers in faith, believers themselves can and do become assured in accordance with the measure of their faith. By this faith they firmly believe that they are and always will remain true and living members of the church, and that they have the forgiveness of sins and eternal life.

Article 10: The Ground of This Assurance

Accordingly, this assurance does not derive from some private revelation beyond or outside the Word but from faith in the promises of God, which are very plentifully revealed in the Word for our comfort, from the testimony of "the Holy Spirit testifying with our spirit that we are God's children and heirs" (Rom. 8:16–17), and finally from a serious and holy pursuit of a clear conscience and of good works. If God's chosen ones in this world did not have this well-founded comfort that the victory will be theirs and this reliable guarantee of eternal glory, they would be of all people most miserable.

Article 11: Doubts concerning This Assurance

Meanwhile, Scripture testifies that believers have to contend in this life with various doubts of the flesh, and that under severe temptation they do not always experience this full assurance of faith and certainty of perseverance. But God, the Father of all comfort, "does not let them be tempted beyond what they can bear, but with the temptation he also provides a way out" (1 Cor. 10:13), and by the Holy Spirit revives in them the assurance of their perseverance.

Article 12: This Assurance as an Incentive to Godliness

This assurance of perseverance, however, so far from making true believers proud and carnally self-assured, is rather the true root of humility, of childlike respect, of genuine godliness, of endurance in every conflict, of fervent prayers, of steadfastness in crossbearing and in confessing the truth, and of well-founded joy in God. Reflecting on this benefit provides an incentive to a serious and continual practice of thanksgiving and good works, as is evident from the testimonies of Scripture and the examples of the saints.

Article 13: Assurance No Inducement to Carelessness

Neither does the renewed confidence of perseverance produce immorality or lack of concern for godliness in those put back on their feet after a fall, but it produces a much greater concern to observe carefully the ways which the Lord prepared in advance. They observe these ways in order that by walking in them they may maintain the assurance of their perseverance, lest, by their abuse of God's fatherly goodness, the face of the gracious God (for the godly, looking upon that face is sweeter than life, but its withdrawal is more bitter than death) turn away from them again, with the result that they fall into greater anguish of spirit.

Article 14: God's Use of Means in Perseverance

And, just as it has pleased God to begin this work of grace in us by the proclamation of the gospel, so God preserves, continues, and completes this work by the hearing and reading of the gospel, by meditation on it, by its exhortations, threats, and promises, and also by the use of the sacraments.

We've already seen that the promise of divine preservation is not a promise of sinful perfection in this life. On the contrary, when we sin in such egregious ways, we "sometimes lose the awareness of grace for a time" (Article 5). God being for us in Christ in a legal sense does not mean he will never frown upon our disobedience as our heavenly Father. But it does mean that God will always effectively renew us to repentance and bring us to "experience again the grace of reconciled God" (5.7). Therefore, we ought to be assured that true believers "are and always will remain true and living members of the church, and that they have the forgiveness of sins and eternal life" (5.9).

In some church traditions—sadly, in some Reformed traditions—it is thought inappropriate, and out of reach for most normal Christians, to have assurance. You can still find churches like this where few people come to the Lord's Table, fearing that they would eat and drink judgment on themselves. Confidence in Christ is something not normally available to the Christian on this side of death. Instead, it can become a mark of real piety to be radically *uncertain* of one's position before the Lord. Anything more would be arrogant presumption.

It's true: assurance is not itself a requirement of true faith. You can be a true Christian and still doubt whether you are a true Christian. We are saved by the object of our faith, that is, Christ, not by the quality of our subjective faith in Christ. Believers contend with doubts in this life and do not always experience this full assurance of faith (Article 11). It's like skating on a frozen pond. Whether you zip onto the ice with great confidence or tiptoe with great uncertainty, it's the thickness of the ice that holds you up, not the fullness of your faith in that ice.

But make no mistake: assurance of perseverance *is* a goal of Christian discipleship. God *wants* us to have confidence, not by presumption, but by faith in his precious promises. "If God's chosen ones in this world did not have this well-founded comfort that the victory will be theirs and this reliable guarantee of eternal glory, they would be of all people most miserable" (Article 10).

But what are the grounds for this assurance? That's the topic under consideration in these articles, and in Article 10 in particular.

In asking that question, Dort is *not* asking about the grounds for our justification or our right standing with God. The question, instead, is about where our assurance of this right standing comes from. Dort asserts, first of all, negatively, that "this assurance does not derive from some private revelation beyond or outside the Word" (5.10). We don't need a dream or a vision from God or some angel to confirm that we are bound for heaven. So if not from external revelation, where, then, does assurance come from? Dort gives three answers:

1. Assurance comes from faith in the promises of God.
2. Assurance comes from the testimony of the Holy Spirit testifying to our spirits that we are children of God.
3. Assurance comes from "a serious and holy pursuit of a clear conscience and of good works" (Article 10).

In short, believers find assurance in the promises of God, the witness of the Spirit, and evidences of Christ's grace in our lives.

This is one of the reasons the perseverance of the saints should never lead to sloth and immorality. When we are confident of the Lord's undying love, "it produces a much greater concern to observe carefully the way of the Lord which he prepared in advance" (Article 13). In fact, we walk in God's ways "in order that by walking them [we] may maintain the assurance of [our] perseverance" (Article 13). As born-again, beloved children we long to know the smile of our gracious God. For "the godly looking upon that face is sweeter than life, but its withdrawal is more bitter than death" (Article 13).

Clearly, Dort believes not only that holiness is a ground for assurance, but that the desire for assurance is itself a motivation unto holiness. Believers should not look *only* to their holy living for assurance, but this should be *one* place they look. When we see evidences of God's grace in us, we should have confidence that God is at work. And he who begins the good work will be faithful to complete it (Phil. 1:6). While we must affirm the continuing imperfection of our obedience, we should not so disregard it that we can no longer find real and assuring evidences of grace at work.

And, finally (for this section), I need to say a few words about Article 14. Notice three things.

First, God works by the hearing of the gospel *and* by the use of the sacraments. We often forget about baptism and the Lord's Supper as means of grace. But they are essential in the cause of gospel confidence. They remind our eyes, our hands, our noses, and our mouths of the good news we hear with our ears.

Second, God causes us to persevere by several means. He makes promises to us, but he also threatens. Imagine taking your child on a trip to the zoo. Before you go, you promise her that there is no reason to be afraid, that you will keep her safe. And how will you keep your little one secure? In part, you may have to threaten her: "Get off that fence. Stay out of the cage. Keep your hands to yourself. Take your head out of its mouth. Listen to me or you will be disciplined." You do whatever you can to keep your child safe. So it is with God. He has not bound himself to one method. Surely this helps us make sense of the warnings in Hebrews and elsewhere in the New Testament. Full-throated threats and exhortations do not undermine perseverance; they help to complete it.

Third, notice the broad way in which Dort understands the gospel (in this context). In a strict sense we might say that the gospel is only the good news of how we can be saved. But in a wider sense, the gospel encompasses the whole story of salvation, which includes not only gospel promises but also the threats and exhortations inherent in the gospel.[1] Sometimes Christians act as if threats and exhortations are all law and no gospel, but Dort reminds us that the good news of God's mercy in Christ is more than a message of unconditional affirmation. God graciously tells us what he's done, what we should do, and what will happen if we plot our own course. All three (promises, threats, exhortation) are instrumental in God's plan to grow us in grace. We should not neglect any of the three in the overall diet of our counseling, preaching, and teaching.

To God Alone Be Glory (Article 15)

Article 15: Contrasting Reactions to the Teaching of Perseverance

This teaching about the perseverance of true believers and saints, and about their assurance of it—a teaching which God has very richly revealed in the Word for the glory of his name and for the comfort of the godly, and which God impresses on the hearts of

---

1. Some older translations of Article 14 connect "exhortations, threatening, and promises" to the "hearing and reading of his Word" instead of to the gospel. That is how the translation adopted by the Christian Reformed Church and included in the 1976 Psalter rendered Article 14 (note: this is the translation used by De Jong in *Crisis in the Reformed Churches* [repr. Grandville, MI: Reformed Fellowship, 2008]). But in the official 1986 version of Dort and in the newest 2011 version produced by the Christian Reformed Church, "exhortations, threats, and promises" are said to belong to the gospel. The original Latin for Article 14 reads: "Quemadmodum autem Deo placuit, opus hoc suum gratiæ per prædicationem Evangelii in nobis inchoare; ita per ejusdem auditum, lectionem, meditationem, adhortationes, minas, promissa, nec non per usum sacramentorum illud conservat, continuat, et perficit" (Phillip Schaff, *Creeds of Christendom*, vol. 3, accessed June 8, 2018, https://www.ccel.org/ccel/schaff/creeds3.iv.xvi.html). One can easily see the Latin word for gospel (*evangelii*). The word *ejusdem* ("of the same") then connects the list that follows back to the gospel. (Thanks to my RTS colleague Blair Smith for providing me with insight into the Latin construction.)

believers—is something that the flesh does not understand, Satan hates, the world ridicules, the ignorant and the hypocrites abuse, and the spirits of error attack. The bride of Christ, on the other hand, has always loved this teaching very tenderly and defended it steadfastly as a priceless treasure; and God, against whom no plan can avail and no strength can prevail, will ensure that the church will continue to do this. To this God alone, Father, Son, and Holy Spirit, be honor and glory forever. Amen.

✳ ✳ ✳

In this last article, Dort explains why the doctrine of the perseverance of true believers is so necessary and so glorious, even though it is sometimes ridiculed and rejected. In the Remonstrance of 1610, the Arminians professed ignorance about whether true believers could finally forfeit grace:

> But whether they can through negligence fall away from the first principle of their life in Christ, again embrace the present world, depart from the pure doctrine once given to them, lose the good conscience, and neglect grace, must first be more carefully determined from the Holy Scriptures before we shall be able to teach this with the full persuasion of our heart.[2]

In other words, we aren't sure what we think, but we certainly cannot commit to the perseverance of the saints.

By 1618, this ambivalence had given way to outright rejection. The Arminians could not accept perseverance based on an absolute decree that had no condition of obedience (*Opinions* D.1). While they believed that God would provide "true believers with as much grace and supernatural powers as he judges, according

---

2. See Remonstrance of 1610 as found in De Jong, *Crisis in the Reformed Churches*, 243–45.

to his infinite wisdom, to be sufficient for persevering," it was still up to man whether he would finally persevere. As such, the Remonstrants affirmed that, "True believers can fall from true faith" (*Opinions* D.3) and that true believers can persevere in "shameful and atrocious deeds" and finally "fall" and "perish" (*Opinions* D.4).

In the end, the Arminians at Dort could offer only an unsure assurance:

> A true believer can and ought indeed to be certain for the future that he is able, by diligent watchfulness, through prayers, and through other holy exercises, to persevere in true faith, and he ought also to be certain that divine grace for persevering will never be lacking; but we do not see how he can be certain that he will never afterwards be remiss in his duty but that he will persevere in faith and in those works of piety and love which are fitting for a believer in this school of Christian warfare; neither do we deem it necessary that concerning this thing a believer should be certain. (*Opinions* D.8)

This leaves the believer in a very tenuous position. He can be certain that God has enough grace to help him persevere, and the believer can be certain that if he does his part, he will persevere. But in the final analysis, the believer cannot be certain that he will actually persevere. This is the logical price one must pay for a commitment to saving faith conditioned upon the choice of the human will from start to finish (see Rejection II).

By contrast, Dort affirms that no plan can avail and no strength can prevail against God (Article 15). And that includes the power of human willing and doing. The golden chain from predestination in eternity, to effectual calling and justification in history, to final glorification in heaven cannot be broken (Rom. 8:30, 37–39). "God's plan cannot be changed; God's promise cannot fail; the calling according to God's purpose cannot be revoked; the merit of Christ as well as his interceding and preserving cannot be nullified; and the sealing of the Holy Spirit can neither be invalidated nor wiped out" (Article 8). We already *have* eternal life (John 5:24). This is one sure reason why those who truly believe will persevere to the end. You cannot be unjustified. You cannot be un-born again. You cannot be lost a second time once you have been found. We will not lose what God has chosen us for in eternity. We will not forfeit what Christ has perfectly accomplished and infallibly applied. We will not, in the end, resist the grace that first entered our lives irresistibly.

This teaching, Dort reminds us, is for "the glory of his name and for the comfort of the godly" (Article 15). Those words could be a banner flying over every article and over every one of the five points. On the other side of Dort's fine-tuned polemics is meant to be this conclusion: God is bigger than we thought, and grace is better than we imagined. If ever there were a "It's not about me!" faith, it should be the Reformed faith. We did not choose to be elect. We did not die for our sins. We did not raise ourselves from the grave. We did not conjure up the miracle of faith. We will not, by our own free will, finish the race. We need a God who does the unconditional electing, a God who does the effectual dying, a God who does the supernatural resurrecting, a God who does the unilateral gifting, and a God who does the unbreakable preserving. That's the grace we need. That's the God we worship. "To this God alone, Father, Son, and Holy Spirit, be honor and glory forever. Amen" (Article 15).

So praise God for old confessions. And praise God for his mercies: planned from eternity and new every morning—unto the very end.

Appendix 1

*Rejection of the Errors by Which the Dutch
Churches Have for Some Time Been Disturbed*

After each Main Point, Dort includes a section called "Rejection of Errors." These sections are compiled here in one document. Dort's positive affirmations cannot be properly understood apart from some knowledge of what Dort is meaning to reject. It's also important to note that most of Dort's scriptural proof texts are found in the Rejection of Errors.

The First Main Point of Doctrine

Having set forth the orthodox teaching concerning election and reprobation, the Synod rejects the errors of those

I

Who teach that the will of God to save those who would believe and persevere in faith and in the obedience of faith is the whole and entire decision of election to salvation, and that nothing else concerning this decision has been revealed in God's Word.

For they deceive the simple and plainly contradict Holy Scripture in its testimony that God does not only wish to save those who would believe, but that he has also from eternity chosen certain particular people to whom, rather than to others, he would within time grant faith in Christ and perseverance. As Scripture says, "I have revealed your name to those whom you gave me" (John 17:6). Likewise, "All who were appointed for eternal life believed" (Acts 13:48), and "He chose us before the foundation of the world so that we should be holy . . ." (Eph. 1:4).

II

Who teach that God's election to eternal life is of many kinds: one general and indefinite, the other particular and definite; and the latter in turn either incomplete, revocable, conditional, or else complete, irrevocable, and absolute. Likewise, who teach that there is one election to faith and another to salvation, so that there can be an election to justifying faith apart from a nonconditional election to salvation.

For this is an invention of the human mind, devised apart from the Scriptures, which distorts the teaching concerning election and breaks up this golden chain of salvation: "Those whom he predestined, he also called; and those whom he called, he also justified; and those whom he justified, he also glorified" (Rom. 8:30).

III

Who teach that God's good pleasure and purpose, which Scripture mentions in its teaching of election, does not involve God's choosing certain particular people rather than others, but involves God's choosing, out of all possible conditions (including the works of the law) or out of the whole order of things, the intrinsically unworthy act of faith, as well as the imperfect obedience of faith, to be a condition of salvation; and it involves his graciously wishing to count this as perfect obedience and to look upon it as worthy of the reward of eternal life.

For by this pernicious error the good pleasure of God and the merit of Christ are robbed of their effectiveness and people are drawn away, by unprofitable inquiries, from the truth of undeserved justification and from the simplicity of the Scriptures. It also gives the lie to these words of the apostle: "God called us with a holy calling, not in virtue of works, but in virtue of his own purpose and the grace which was given to us in Christ Jesus before the beginning of time" (2 Tim. 1:9).

IV

Who teach that in election to faith a prerequisite condition is that humans should rightly use the light of nature, be upright, unassuming, humble, and disposed to eternal life, as though election depended to some extent on these factors.

For this smacks of Pelagius, and it clearly calls into question the words of the apostle: "We lived at one time in the passions of our flesh, following the will of our flesh and thoughts, and we were by nature children of wrath, like everyone else. But God, who is rich in mercy, out of the great love with which he loved us, even when we were dead in transgressions, made us alive with Christ, by whose grace you have been saved. And God raised us up with him and seated us with him in heaven in Christ Jesus, in order that in the coming ages we might show the surpassing riches of his grace, according to his kindness toward us in Christ Jesus. For it is by grace you have been saved, through faith (and this not from yourselves; it is the gift of God) not by works, so that no one can boast" (Eph. 2:3–9).

V

Who teach that the incomplete and conditional election of particular persons to salvation occurred on the basis of a foreseen faith, repentance, holiness, and godliness, which has just begun or continued for some time; but that complete and nonconditional election occurred on the basis of a foreseen perseverance to the end in faith, repentance, holiness, and godliness. And that this is the gracious and evangelical worthiness, on account of which the one who is chosen is more worthy than the one who is not chosen. And therefore that faith, the obedience of faith, holiness, godliness, and perseverance are not fruits or effects of an unchangeable election to glory, but indispensable conditions and causes, which are prerequisite in those who are to be chosen in the complete election, and which are foreseen as achieved in them.

This runs counter to the entire Scripture, which throughout impresses upon our ears and hearts these sayings among others: "Election is not by works, but by him who calls" (Rom. 9:11–12); "All who were appointed for eternal life believed" (Acts 13:48); "He chose us in himself so that we should be holy" (Eph. 1:4); "You did not choose me, but I chose you" (John 15:26); "If by grace, not by works" (Rom. 11:6); "In this is love, not that we loved God, but that he loved us and sent his Son" (1 John 4:10).

VI

Who teach that not every election to salvation is unchangeable, but that some of the chosen can perish and do in fact perish eternally, with no decision of God to prevent it.

By this gross error they make God changeable, destroy the comfort of the godly concerning the steadfastness of their election, and contradict the Holy Scriptures, which teach that "the elect cannot be led astray" (Matt. 24:24), that "Christ does not lose those given to him by the Father" (John 6:39), and that "those whom God predestined, called, and justified, he also glorifies" (Rom. 8:30).

VII

Who teach that in this life there is no fruit, no awareness, and no assurance of one's unchangeable election to glory, except as conditioned upon something changeable and contingent.

For not only is it absurd to speak of an uncertain assurance, but these things also militate against the experience of the saints, who with the apostle rejoice from an awareness of their election and sing the praises of this gift of God; who, as Christ urged, "rejoice" with his disciples "that their names have been written in heaven" (Luke 10:20); and finally who hold up against the flaming arrows of the devil's temptations the awareness of their election, with the question "Who will bring any charge against those whom God has chosen?" (Rom. 8:33).

VIII

Who teach that it was not on the basis of his just will alone that God decided to leave anyone in the fall of Adam and in the common state of sin and condemnation or to pass anyone by in the imparting of grace necessary for faith and conversion.

For these words stand fast: "He has mercy on whom he wishes, and he hardens whom he wishes" (Rom. 9:18). And also: "To you it has been given to know the secrets of the kingdom of heaven, but to them it has not been given" (Matt. 13:11). Likewise: "I give glory to you, Father, Lord of heaven and earth, that you have hidden these things from the wise and understanding, and have revealed them to little children; yes, Father, because that was your pleasure" (Matt. 11:25–26).

IX

Who teach that the cause for God's sending the gospel to one people rather than to another is not merely and solely God's good pleasure, but rather that one people is better and worthier than the other to whom the gospel is not communicated.

For Moses contradicts this when he addresses the people of Israel as follows: "Behold, to Jehovah your God belong the heavens and the highest heavens, the earth and whatever is in it. But Jehovah was inclined in his affection to love your ancestors alone, and chose out their descendants after them, you above all peoples, as at this day" (Deut. 10:14–15). And also Christ: "Woe to you, Korazin! Woe to you, Bethsaida! for if those mighty works done in you had been done in Tyre and Sidon, they would have repented long ago in sackcloth and ashes" (Matt. 11:21).

The Second Main Point of Doctrine

Having set forth the orthodox teaching, the Synod rejects the errors of those

I

Who teach that God the Father appointed his Son to death on the cross without a fixed and definite plan to save anyone by name, so that the necessity, usefulness, and worth of what Christ's death obtained could have stood intact and altogether perfect, complete and whole, even if the redemption that was obtained had never in actual fact been applied to any individual.

For this assertion is an insult to the wisdom of God the Father and to the merit of Jesus Christ, and it is contrary to Scripture. For the Savior speaks as follows: "I lay down my life for the sheep, and I know them" (John 10:15, 27). And Isaiah the prophet says concerning the Savior: "When he shall make himself an offering for sin, he shall see his offspring, he shall prolong his days, and the will of Jehovah shall prosper in his hand" (Isa. 53:10). Finally, this undermines the article of the creed in which we confess what we believe concerning the Church.

II

Who teach that the purpose of Christ's death was not to establish in actual fact a new covenant of grace by his blood, but only to acquire for the Father the mere right to enter once more into a covenant with humanity, whether of grace or of works.

For this conflicts with Scripture, which teaches that Christ "has become the guarantee and mediator" of a better—that is, a new—covenant (Heb. 7:22; 9:15), "and that a will is in force only when someone has died" (Heb. 9:17).

III

Who teach that Christ, by the satisfaction which he gave, did not certainly merit for anyone salvation itself and the faith by which this satisfaction of Christ is effectively applied to salvation, but only acquired for the Father the authority or plenary will to relate in a new way with humanity and to impose such new conditions as he chose, and that the satisfying of these conditions depends on human free choice; consequently, that it was possible that either all or none would fulfill them.

For they have too low an opinion of the death of Christ, do not at all acknowledge the foremost fruit or benefit which it brings forth, and summon back from hell the Pelagian error.

IV

Who teach that what is involved in the new covenant of grace which God the Father made with humanity through the intervening of Christ's death is not that we are justified before God and saved through faith, insofar as it accepts Christ's merit, but rather that God, having withdrawn his demand for perfect obedience to the law, counts faith itself, and the imperfect obedience of faith, as perfect obedience to the law, and graciously looks upon this as worthy of the reward of eternal life.

For they contradict Scripture: "They are justified freely by his grace through the redemption that came by Jesus Christ, whom God presented as a sacrifice of atonement, through faith in his blood" (Rom. 3:24–25). And along with the ungodly Socinus, they introduce a new and foreign justification of humanity before God, against the consensus of the whole church.

V

Who teach that all people have been received into the state of reconciliation and into the grace of the covenant, so that no one on account of original sin is liable to condemnation, or is to be condemned, but that all are free from the guilt of this sin.

For this opinion conflicts with Scripture which asserts that we are by nature children of wrath.

VI

Who make use of the distinction between obtaining and applying in order to instill in the unwary and inexperienced the opinion that God, as far as he is concerned, wished to bestow equally upon all people the benefits which are gained by Christ's death; but that the distinction by which some rather than others come to share in the forgiveness of sins and eternal life depends on their own free choice (which applies itself to the grace offered indiscriminately) but does not depend on the unique gift of mercy which effectively works in them, so that they, rather than others, apply that grace to themselves.

For, while pretending to set forth this distinction in an acceptable sense, they attempt to give the people the deadly poison of Pelagianism.

VII

Who teach that Christ neither could die, nor had to die, nor did die for those whom God so dearly loved and chose to eternal life, since such people do not need the death of Christ.

For they contradict the apostle, who says: "Christ loved me and gave himself up for me" (Gal. 2:20), and likewise: "Who will bring any charge against those whom God has chosen? It is God who justifies. Who is he that condemns? It is Christ who died," that is, for them (Rom. 8:33–34). They also contradict the Savior, who asserts: "I lay down my life for the sheep" (John 10:15), and "My command is this: Love one another as I have loved you. Greater love has no one than this, that one lay down his life for one's friends" (John 15:12–13).

The Third and Fourth Main Points of Doctrine

Having set forth the orthodox teaching, the Synod rejects the errors of those

I

Who teach that, properly speaking, it cannot be said that original sin in itself is enough to condemn the whole human race or to warrant temporal and eternal punishments.

For they contradict the apostle when he says: "Sin entered the world through one man, and death through sin, and in this way death passed on to all people because all sinned" (Rom. 5:12); also: "The guilt followed one sin and brought condemnation" (Rom. 5:16); likewise: "The wages of sin is death" (Rom. 6:23).

II

Who teach that the spiritual gifts or the good dispositions and virtues such as goodness, holiness, and righteousness could not have resided in the human will at creation, and therefore could not have been separated from the will at the fall.

For this conflicts with the apostle's description of the image of God in Ephesians 4:24, where he portrays the image in terms of righteousness and holiness, which definitely reside in the will.

III

Who teach that in spiritual death the spiritual gifts have not been separated from human will, since the will in itself has never been corrupted but only hindered by the darkness of the mind and the unruliness of the emotions, and since the will is able to exercise its innate free capacity once these hindrances are removed, which is to say, it is able of itself to will or choose whatever good is set before it—or else not to will or choose it.

This is a novel idea and an error and has the effect of elevating the power of free choice, contrary to the words of Jeremiah the prophet: "The heart itself is deceitful above all things and wicked" (Jer. 17:9); and of the words of the apostle: "All of us also lived among them" (the children of disobedience) "at one time in the passions of our flesh, following the will of our flesh and thoughts" (Eph. 2:3).

IV

Who teach that unregenerate humanity is not strictly or totally dead in sin or deprived of all capacity for spiritual good but is able to hunger and thirst for righteousness or life and to offer the sacrifice of a broken and contrite spirit which is pleasing to God.

For these views are opposed to the plain testimonies of Scripture: "You were dead in your transgressions and sins" (Eph. 2:1, 5);

"The imagination of the thoughts of the human heart is only evil all the time" (Gen. 6:5; 8:21). Besides, to hunger and thirst for deliverance from misery and for life, and to offer God the sacrifice of a broken spirit is characteristic only of the regenerate and of those called blessed (Ps. 51:17; Matt. 5:6).

V

Who teach that corrupt and natural humanity can make such good use of common grace (by which they mean the light of nature) or of the gifts remaining after the fall that they are able thereby gradually to obtain a greater grace—evangelical or saving grace—as well as salvation itself; and that in this way God, for his part, shows himself ready to reveal Christ to all people, since God provides to all, to a sufficient extent and in an effective manner, the means necessary for the revealing of Christ, for faith, and for repentance.

For Scripture, not to mention the experience of all ages, testifies that this is false: "He makes known his words to Jacob, his statutes and his laws to Israel; he has done this for no other nation, and they do not know his laws" (Ps. 147:19–20); "In the past God let all nations go their own way" (Acts 14:16); "They" (Paul and his companions) "were kept by the Holy Spirit from speaking God's word in Asia"; and "When they had come to Mysia, they tried to go to Bithynia, but the Spirit would not allow them to" (Acts 16:6–7).

VI

Who teach that in the true conversion of men and women new qualities, dispositions, or gifts cannot be infused or poured into their will by God, and indeed that the faith [or believing] by which we first come to conversion and from which we receive the name "believers" is not a quality or gift infused by God, but only a human act, and that it cannot be called a gift except in respect to the power of attaining faith.

For these views contradict the Holy Scriptures, which testify that God does infuse or pour into our hearts the new qualities of faith, obedience, and the experiencing of his love: "I will put my law in their minds, and write it on their hearts" (Jer. 31:33); "I will pour water on the thirsty land, and streams on the dry ground; I will pour out my Spirit on your offspring" (Isa. 44:3); "The love of God has been poured out in our hearts by the Holy Spirit, who has been given to us" (Rom. 5:5). They also conflict with the continuous practice of the Church, which prays with the prophet: "Convert me, Lord, and I shall be converted" (Jer. 31:18).

VII

Who teach that the grace by which we are converted to God is nothing but a gentle persuasion, or (as others explain it) that the way of God's acting in conversion that is most noble and suited to human nature is that which happens by persuasion, and that nothing prevents this grace of moral persuasion even by itself from making the natural person spiritual; indeed, that God does not produce the assent of the will except in this manner of moral persuasion, and that the effectiveness of God's work by which it surpasses the work of Satan consists in the fact that God promises eternal benefits while Satan promises temporal ones.

For this teaching is entirely Pelagian and contrary to the whole of Scripture, which recognizes besides this persuasion also another, far more effective and divine way in which the Holy Spirit acts in human conversion. As Ezekiel 36:26 puts it: "I will give you a new heart and put a new spirit in you; and I will remove your heart of stone and give you a heart of flesh."

VIII

Who teach that God in regenerating people does not bring to bear that power of his omnipotence whereby God may powerfully and unfailingly bend the human will to faith and conversion, but that even when God has accomplished all the works of grace which he uses for their conversion, they nevertheless can, and in actual fact often do, so resist God and the Spirit in their intent and will to regenerate them, that they completely thwart their own rebirth; and, indeed, that it remains in their own power whether or not to be reborn.

For this does away with all effective functioning of God's grace in our conversion and subjects the activity of Almighty God to human will; it is contrary to the apostles, who teach that "we believe by virtue of the effective working of God's mighty strength" (Eph. 1:19), and that "God fulfills the undeserved good will of his kindness and the work of faith in us with power" (2 Thess. 1:11), and likewise that "his divine power has given us everything we need for life and godliness" (2 Pet. 1:3).

IX

Who teach that grace and free choice are concurrent partial causes which cooperate to initiate conversion, and that grace does not precede—in the order of causality—the effective influence of the will; that is to say, that God does not effectively help the human will to come to conversion before that will itself motivates and determines itself.

For the early church already condemned this doctrine long ago in the Pelagians, on the basis of the words of the apostle: "It does not depend on human willing or running but on God's mercy" (Rom. 9:16); also: "Who makes you different from anyone else?" and "What do you have that you did not receive?" (1 Cor. 4:7);

likewise: "It is God who works in you to will and act according to his good pleasure" (Phil. 2:13).

The Fifth Main Point of Doctrine

Having set forth the orthodox teaching, the Synod rejects the errors of those

I

Who teach that the perseverance of true believers is not an effect of election or a gift of God produced by Christ's death, but a condition of the new covenant which people, before what they call their "peremptory" election and justification, must fulfill by their free will.

For Holy Scripture testifies that perseverance follows from election and is granted to the chosen by virtue of Christ's death, resurrection, and intercession: "The chosen obtained it; the others were hardened" (Rom. 11:7); likewise, "He who did not spare his own son, but gave him up for us all—how will he not, along with him, grant us all things? Who will bring any charge against those whom God has chosen? It is God who justifies. Who is he that condemns? It is Christ Jesus who died—more than that, who was raised—who also sits at the right hand of God, and is also interceding for us. Who shall separate us from the love of Christ?" (Rom. 8:32–35).

II

Who teach that God does provide believers with sufficient strength to persevere and is ready to preserve this strength in them if they perform their duty, but that even with all those things in place which are necessary to persevere in faith and which God is pleased to use to preserve faith, it still always depends on the choice of human will whether or not to persevere.

For this view is obviously Pelagian; and though it intends to make people free it makes them sacrilegious. It is against the enduring consensus of evangelical teaching which takes from humanity all cause for boasting and ascribes the praise for this benefit only to God's grace. It is also against the testimony of the apostle: "It is God who keeps us strong to the end, so that we will be blameless on the day of our Lord Jesus Christ" (1 Cor. 1:8).

III

Who teach that those who truly believe and have been born again not only can forfeit justifying faith as well as grace and salvation totally and to the end, but also in actual fact do often forfeit them and are lost forever.

For this opinion nullifies the very grace of justification and regeneration as well as the continual preservation by Christ, contrary to the plain words of the apostle Paul: "If Christ died for us while we were still sinners, we will therefore much more be saved from God's wrath through him, since we have now been justified by his blood" (Rom. 5:8–9); and contrary to the apostle John: "No one who is born of God is intent on sin, because God's seed remains in him, nor can he sin, because he has been born of God" (1 John 3:9); also contrary to the words of Jesus Christ: "I give eternal life to my sheep, and they shall never perish; no one can snatch them out of my hand. My Father, who has given them to me, is greater than all; no one can snatch them out of my Father's hand" (John 10:28–29).

IV

Who teach that those who truly believe and have been born again can commit the sin that leads to death (the sin against the Holy Spirit).

For the same apostle John, after making mention of those who commit the sin that leads to death and forbidding prayer for them

(1 John 5:16–17), immediately adds: "We know that anyone born of God does not commit sin" (that is, that kind of sin), "but the one who was born of God keeps himself safe, and the evil one does not touch him" (v. 18).

V

Who teach that apart from a special revelation no one can have the assurance of future perseverance in this life.

For by this teaching the well-founded consolation of true believers in this life is taken away and the doubting of the Romanists is reintroduced into the church. Holy Scripture, however, in many places derives the assurance not from a special and extraordinary revelation but from the marks peculiar to God's children and from God's completely reliable promises. So especially the apostle Paul: "Nothing in all creation can separate us from the love of God that is in Christ Jesus our Lord" (Rom. 8:39); and John: "They who obey his commands remain in him and he in them. And this is how we know that he remains in us: by the Spirit he gave us" (1 John 3:24).

VI

Who teach that the teaching of the assurance of perseverance and of salvation is by its very nature and character an opiate of the flesh and is harmful to godliness, good morals, prayer, and other holy exercises, but that, on the contrary, to have doubt about this is praiseworthy.

For these people show that they do not know the effective operation of God's grace and the work of the indwelling Holy Spirit, and they contradict the apostle John, who asserts the opposite in plain words: "Dear friends, now we are children of God, but what we will be has not yet been made known. But we know that when he is made known, we shall be like him, for we shall see him as he is. Everyone who has this hope in him purifies himself, just as he is pure" (1 John 3:2–3). Moreover, they are refuted by the examples of the saints in both the Old and the New Testament, who though assured of their perseverance and salvation yet were constant in prayer and other exercises of godliness.

VII

Who teach that the faith of those who believe only temporarily does not differ from justifying and saving faith except in duration alone.

For Christ himself in Matthew 13:20ff. and Luke 8:13ff. clearly defines these further differences between temporary and true believers: he says that the former receive the seed on rocky ground, and the latter receive it in good ground, or a good heart; the former have no root, and the latter are firmly rooted; the former have no fruit, and the latter produce fruit in varying measure, with steadfastness, or perseverance.

VIII

Who teach that it is not absurd that people, after losing their former regeneration, should once again, indeed quite often, be reborn.

For by this teaching they deny the imperishable nature of God's seed by which we are born again, contrary to the testimony of the apostle Peter: "Born again, not of perishable seed, but of imperishable" (1 Pet. 1:23).

IX

Who teach that Christ nowhere prayed for an unfailing perseverance of believers in faith.

For they contradict Christ himself when he says: "I have prayed for you, Peter, that your faith may not fail" (Luke 22:32); and John the gospel writer when he testifies in John 17 that it was not only for the apostles, but also for all those who were to believe by their message that Christ prayed: "Holy Father, preserve them in your name" (v. 11); and "My prayer is not that you take them out of the world, but that you preserve them from the evil one" (v. 15).

Appendix 2

Conclusion: Rejection of False Accusations

After the final Rejection of Errors comes this last section on false accusations. We see here Dort's desire to defend Reformed theology from slander and to call upon Christ to protect the truth and sanctify his church.·

And so this is the clear, simple, and straightforward explanation of the orthodox teaching on the five articles in dispute in the Netherlands, as well as the rejection of the errors by which the Dutch churches have for some time been disturbed. This explanation and rejection the Synod declares to be derived from God's Word and in agreement with the confessions of the Reformed churches. Hence it clearly appears that those of whom one could hardly expect it have shown no truth, equity, and charity at all in wishing to make the public believe:

- that the teaching of the Reformed churches on predestination and on the points associated with it by its very nature and tendency draws the minds of people away from all godliness and religion, is an opiate of the flesh and the devil, and is a stronghold where Satan lies in wait for all people, wounds most of them, and fatally pierces many of them with the arrows of both despair and self-assurance;

- that this teaching makes God the author of sin, unjust, a tyrant, and a hypocrite; and is nothing but a refurbished Stoicism, Manicheism, Libertinism, and Turkism [i.e. Islam];

- that this teaching makes people carnally self-assured, since it persuades them that nothing endangers the salvation of the elect, no matter how they live, so that they may commit the most outrageous crimes with self-assurance; and that on the other hand nothing is of use to the reprobate for salvation even if they have truly performed all the works of the saints;

- that this teaching means that God predestined and created, by the bare and unqualified choice of his will, without the least regard or consideration of any sin, the greatest part of the world to eternal condemnation; that in the same manner in which election is the source and cause of faith and good works, reprobation is the cause of unbelief and ungodliness; that many infant children of believers are snatched in their innocence from their mothers' breasts and cruelly cast into hell so that neither the blood of Christ nor their baptism nor the prayers of the church at their baptism can be of any use to them; and very many other slanderous accusations of this kind which the Reformed churches not only disavow but even denounce with their whole heart.

Therefore this Synod of Dort in the name of the Lord pleads with all who devoutly call on the name of our Savior Jesus Christ to form their judgment about the faith of the Reformed churches, not on the basis of false accusations gathered from here or there, or even on the basis of the personal statements of a number of ancient and modern authorities—statements which are also often either quoted out of context or misquoted and twisted to convey a different meaning—but on the basis of the churches' own official confessions and of the present explanation of the orthodox teaching which has been endorsed by the unanimous consent of the members of the whole Synod, one and all.

Moreover, the Synod earnestly warns the false accusers themselves to consider how heavy a judgment of God awaits those who give false testimony against so many churches and their confessions, trouble the consciences of the weak, and seek to prejudice the minds of many against the fellowship of true believers.

Finally, this Synod urges all fellow ministers in the gospel of Christ to deal with this teaching in a godly and reverent manner, in the academic institutions as well as in the churches; to do so, both in their speaking and writing, with a view to the glory of God's name, holiness of life, and the comfort of anxious souls; to think and also speak with Scripture according to the analogy of faith; and, finally, to refrain from all those ways of speaking which go beyond the bounds set for us by the genuine sense of the Holy Scriptures and which could give impertinent sophists a just occasion to scoff at the teaching of the Reformed churches or even to bring false accusations against it.

May God's Son Jesus Christ, who sits at the right hand of God and gives gifts to humanity, sanctify us in the truth, lead to the truth those who err, silence the mouths of those who lay false accusations against sound teaching, and equip faithful ministers of God's Word with a spirit of wisdom and discretion, that all they say may be to the glory of God and the building up of their hearers. Amen.

Appendix 3

The Opinions of the Remonstrants (1618)

During the Synod of Dort, the Remonstrants were summoned to appear and to state their convictions on the disputed points of doctrine. They presented their opinions on the first article on December 13 and their opinions on the other articles on December 17. The text below is taken from "Appendix H" in *Crisis in the Reformed Churches*, ed. Peter Y. De Jong (Middleville, MI: Reformed Fellowship, 2008), pp. 261–68, and is used with permission of Reformed Fellowship Inc. (Note: Article C.12 is mistakenly labeled as C.13 in De Jong; I've used the proper sequencing).

A. The Opinion of the Remonstrants regarding the first article, dealing with the decree of Predestination.

1. God has not decided to elect anyone to eternal life, or to reject anyone from the same, prior to the decree to create him, without any consideration of preceding obedience or disobedience, according to His good pleasure, for the

demonstration of the glory of His mercy and justice, or of His absolute power and dominion.

2. Since the decree of God concerning both the salvation and perdition of each man is not a decree of the end absolutely intended, it follows that neither are such means subordinated to that same decree by which the elect and the reprobate are efficaciously and inevitably led to their final destination.

3. Therefore God has not with this plan created in the one Adam all men in a state of rectitude, has not ordained the fall and the permission of it, has not withdrawn from Adam the grace which was necessary and sufficient, has not brought it about that the Gospel is preached and that men are externally called, does not confer on them any gifts of the Holy Spirit by means of which he leads some of them to life, but deprives others of the benefit of life, Christ, the Mediator, is not solely the executor of election, but also the foundation of that same decree of election: the reason why some are efficaciously called, justified, persevere in faith, and are glorified is not that they have been absolutely elected to eternal life. That others are left in the fall, that Christ is not given to them, that they are either not called at all or not efficaciously called—these are not the reasons why they are absolutely rejected from eternal salvation.

4. God has not decreed to leave the greatest part of men in the fall, excluded from every hope of salvation, apart from intervening actual sins.

5. God has ordained that Christ should be a propitiation for the sins of the whole world, and by virtue of that decree

He has determined to justify and to save those who believe in Him, and to provide for men means necessary and sufficient for faith in such a way as He knows to be in harmony with His wisdom and justice. But He has by no means determined, by virtue of an absolute decree, to give Christ the Mediator solely to the elect, and through an efficacious calling to bestow faith upon, justify, preserve in the faith and glorify them alone.

6. No one is rejected from life nor from the means sufficient for it by an absolute antecedent decree, so that the merit of Christ, calling, and all the gifts of the Spirit can be profitable to salvation for all, and truly are, unless they themselves by the abuse of these gifts pervert them to their own perdition; but to unbelief, to impiety, and to sins, a means and causes of damnation, no one is predestined.

7. The election of particular persons is decisive, out of consideration of faith in Jesus Christ and of perseverance; not, however, apart from a consideration of faith and perseverance in the true faith, as a condition prerequisite for electing.

8. Rejection from eternal life is made on the basis of a consideration of antecedent unbelief and perseverance in unbelief; not, however, apart from a consideration of antecedent unbelief and perseverance in unbelief.

9. All the children of believers are sanctified in Christ, so that no one of them who leaves this life before the use of reason will perish. By no means, however, are to be considered among the number of the reprobate certain children of believers who leave this life in infancy before they have committed any actual sin in their own persons, so that neither

the holy bath of baptism nor the prayers of the church for them in any way be profitable for their salvation.

10. No children of believers who have been baptized in the name of the Father, the Son, and the Holy Spirit, living in the state of infancy, are reckoned among the reprobate by an absolute decree.

B. The Opinion of the Remonstrants regarding the second article, which deals with the universality of the merit of the death of Christ.

1. The price of redemption which Christ offered to God the Father is not only in itself and by itself sufficient for the redemption of the whole human race but has also been paid for all men and for every man, according to the decree, will, and the grace of God the Father; therefore no one is absolutely excluded from participation in the fruits of Christ's death by an absolute and antecedent decree of God.

2. Christ has, by the merit of his death, so reconciled God the Father to the whole human race that the Father, on account of that merit, without giving up His righteousness and truth, has been able and has willed to make and confirm a new covenant of grace with sinners and men liable to damnation.

3. Though Christ has merited reconciliation with God and remission of sins for all men and for every man, yet no one, according to the pact of the new and gracious covenant, becomes a true partaker of the benefits obtained by the death of Christ in any other way than by faith; nor are sins forgiven to sinning men before they actually and truly believe in Christ.

4. Only those are obliged to believe that Christ died for them for whom Christ has died. The reprobates, however, as they are called, for whom Christ has not died, are not obligated to such faith, nor can they be justly condemned on account of the contrary refusal to believe this. In fact, if there should be such reprobates, they would be obliged to believe that Christ has not died for them.

C. The Opinion of the Remonstrants regarding the third and fourth articles, concerning the grace of God and the conversion of man.

1. Man does not have saving faith of himself, nor out of the powers of his free will, since in the state of sin he is able of himself and by himself neither to think, will, or do any good (which would indeed to be saving good, the most prominent of which is saving faith). It is necessary therefore that by God in Christ through His Holy Spirit he be regenerated and renewed in intellect, affections, will, and in all his powers, so that he might be able to understand, reflect upon, will and carry out the good things which pertain to salvation.

2. We hold, however, that the grace of God is not only the beginning but also the progression and the completion of every good, so much so that even the regenerate himself is unable to think, will, or do the good, or to resist any temptations to evil, apart from that preceding or prevenient, awakening, following and cooperating grace. Hence all good works and actions which anyone by cogitation is able to comprehend are to be ascribed to the grace of God.

3. Yet we do not believe that all zeal, care, and diligence applied to the obtaining of salvation before faith itself and the

Spirit of renewal are vain and ineffectual—indeed, rather harmful to man than useful and fruitful. On the contrary, we hold that to hear the Word of God, to be sorry for sins committed, to desire saving grace and the Spirit of renewal (none of which things man is able to do without grace) are not only not harmful and useless, but rather most useful and most necessary for the obtaining of faith and of the Spirit of renewal.

4. The will in the fallen state, before calling, does not have the power and the freedom to will any saving good. And therefore we deny that the freedom to will saving good as well as evil is present to the will in every state.

5. The efficacious grace by which anyone is converted is not irresistible; and though God so influences the will by the word and the internal operation of His Spirit that he both confers the strength to believe or supernatural powers, and actually causes man to believe—yet man is able of himself to despise that grace and not to believe, and therefore to perish through his own fault.

6. Although according to the most free will of God the disparity of divine grace is very great, nevertheless, the Holy Spirit confers, or is ready to confer, as much grace to all men and to each man to whom the Word of God is preached as is sufficient for promoting the conversion of men in its steps. Therefore sufficient grace for faith and conversion falls to the lot not only of those whom God is said to will to save according to the decree of absolute election, but also of those who are not actually converted.

7. Man is able through the grace of the Holy Spirit to do more good than he actually does, and to avoid more evil than

he actually avoids; and we do not believe that God simply does not will that man should do more good than he does and avoid more evil than he does avoid, and that God has decreed precisely from eternity that both should so happen.

8. Whomever God calls to salvation, he calls seriously, that is, with a sincere and completely unhypocritical intention and will to save; nor do we assent to the opinion of those who hold that God calls certain ones externally whom He does not will to call internally, that is, as truly converted, even before the grace of calling has been rejected.

9. There is not in God a secret will which so contradicts the will of the same revealed in the Word that according to it (that is, the secret will) He does not will the conversion and salvation of the greatest part of those whom He seriously calls and invites by the Word of the Gospel and by His revealed will; and we do not here, as some say, acknowledge in God a holy simulation, or a double person.

10. Nor do we believe that God calls the reprobate, as they are called, to these ends: that He should the more harden them, or take away excuse, or punish them the more severely, or display their inability; nor, however, that they should be converted, should believe, and should be saved.

11. It is not true that all things, not only good but also bad, necessarily occur, from the power and efficacy of the secret will or decree of God, and that indeed those who sin, out of consideration of the decree of God, are not able to sin; that God wills to determine and to bring about the sins of men, their insane, foolish, and cruel works, and the sacrilegious blasphemy of His name—in fact, to move the tongues of men to blasphemy, and so on.

12. To us the following is false and horrible: that God impels men to sins which He openly prohibits; that those who sin do not act contrary to the will of God properly named; that what is unrighteous (that is, what is contrary to the will of God properly named); that what is unrighteous (that is, what is contrary to His precept) is in agreement with the will of God; indeed, that it is truly a capital crime to do the will of God.

D. The Opinion of the Remonstrants with respect to the fifth article, which concerns Perseverance.

1. The perseverance of believers in the faith is not an effect of the absolute decree by which God is said to have chosen singular persons defined by no condition of obedience.

2. God provides true believers with as much grace and supernatural powers as He judges, according to His infinite wisdom, to be sufficient for persevering and for overcoming the temptations of the devil, the flesh, and the world; it is never charged to God's account that they do not persevere.

3. True believers can fall from true faith and can fall into such sins as cannot be consistent with true and justifying faith; not only is it possible for this to happen, but it even happens frequently.

4. True believers are able to fall through their own fault into shameful and atrocious deeds, to persevere and to die in them; and therefore finally to fall and to perish.

5. Nevertheless we do not believe that true believers, though they may sometimes fall into grave sins which are vexing to their consciences, immediately fall out of every hope of repentance; but we acknowledge that it can happen that

God, according to the multitude of His mercies, may recall them through His grace to repentance; in fact, we believe that this happens not infrequently, although we cannot be persuaded that this will certainly and indubitably happen.

6. The following dogmas, therefore, which by public writings are being scattered among the people, we reject with our whole mind and heart as harmful to piety and good morals: namely, (1) True believers are not able to sin deliberately, but only out of ignorance and weakness. (2) True believers through no sins can fall out of the grace of God. (3) A thousand sins, even all the sins of the whole world, are not able to render election invalid . . . (4) To believers and to the elect no sins, however great and grave they can be, are imputed; but all present and future sins have already been remitted. (5) True believers, having fallen into destructive heresies, into grave and most atrocious sins, like adultery and homicide, on account of which the church, after the justification of Christ, is compelled to testify that it is not able to tolerate them in its external communion and that they will have no part in the kingdom of Christ unless they are converted, nevertheless are not able to fall from faith totally and finally.

7. A true believer, as for the present time he can be certain about his faith and the integrity of his conscience, and thus also concerning his salvation and the saving benevolence of God toward him, for that time can be and ought to be certain; and on this point we reject the pontifical opinion.

8. A true believer can and ought indeed to be certain for the future that he is able, by diligent watchfulness, through prayers, and through other holy exercises, to persevere in true faith, and he ought also to be certain that divine

grace for persevering will never be lacking; but we do not see how he can be certain that he will never afterwards be remiss in his duty but that he will persevere in faith and in those works of piety and love which are fitting for a believer in this school of Christian warfare; neither do we deem it necessary that concerning this thing a believer should be certain.

Appendix 4

Scripture Proofs in the Canons of Dort

While this book is not intended to be a scriptural defense of Reformed soteriology, the canons themselves provide plenty of biblical support for the five main points of doctrine. The eager student, alone or with others, would do well to study the passages cited by Dort, most of which come from the Rejection of Errors at the end of each main point.

Election and Reprobation

Deuteronomy 10:14–15; Matthew 11:21, 25–26; 13:11; 24:24; Luke 10:20; John 3:16; 6:39; 17:6; Acts 13:48; 15:18; Romans 3:19; 3:23; 6:23; 8:30, 33; 9:11–13, 18; 10:14–15; 11:6, 33–36; Ephesians 1:4–6, 11; 2:3–9; 2:8; Philippians 1:29; 2 Timothy 1:9; 1 John 4:9, 10

Christ's Death and Human Redemption through It

Isaiah 53:10; John 10:15, 27; 15:12–13; Romans 3:24–25; 8:33–34; Galatians 2:20; Hebrews 7:22; 9:15, 17

Human Corruption

Genesis 6:5; 8:21; Psalm 51:17; 147:19-20; Jeremiah 17:9; Matthew 5:6; 13; Acts 14:6; 16:6–7; Romans 5:12, 16; 6:23; Ephesians 2:1, 3, 5; 4:24

Conversion to God

Isaiah 44:3; Jeremiah 31:18, 33; Ezekiel 36:26; Romans 5:5; 9:16; 1 Corinthians 4:7; Ephesians 1:19; Philippians 2:13; 2 Thessalonians 1:11; 2 Peter 1:3

Perseverance of the Saints

Matthew 13:20ff.; Luke 8:13ff.; 22:32; John 10:28–29; 17:11, 15; Romans 5:8–9; 8:16–17, 32–35, 39; 11:7; 1 Corinthians 1:8; 10:13; 1 Peter 1:23; 1 John 3:2–3, 9, 24; 5:16–17, 18

General Index

Adam, 29, 65–66, 101, 120
adoption, 33–34, 36, 84, 86
affections, 36, 65n, 102, 123. *See
also* emotions
"And Can It Be," 74
Anglican church, 60
apostles, 40, 68, 71, 76–77, 109,
114; John, 112; Paul, 29, 33,
41–42, 68, 99, 101, 105–6,
109, 111–12; Peter, 109, 113
Aquinas, Thomas, 50
Arminian theology: conversion,
63–64, 67, 69, 73–74, 123–26;
election, 27–28, 35–36, 43,
119–22; history of, 15–25,
47–48; perseverance, 93–95,
126–28; redemption, 54–62,
122–23
Arminius, Jacobus, 15–18, 21
assurance: comfort of, 25, 32, 40,
44, 87, 90, 92, 95, 100, 117;
doubts and, 40–41, 87–90,
101, 112; effects of, 38–39,
87–88, 90, 101; is harmful to
obedience, 38, 45, 112–13,
116; is helpful to obedience,
38, 88, 90–91, 113; reac-
tions to teaching of, 92–93,
101, 112, 115; self-assurance,
38–39, 45, 69, 76, 88, 116.
See also Canons of Dort, Fifth
Main Point

atonement: definite, 14, 32, 35–36,
47–62, 73, 98, 102; effectual,
52, 56, 61, 79, 95; extent of,
47–48, 57–61, 107; God's will
and, 51, 53, 56–57, 60n, 61n,
125; indefinite, 60, 98; limited,
14, 19, 47–62; nature of, 47–51,
57, 61; universal, 53–54, 59n,
60–61, 122. *See also* Canons of
Dort, Second Main Point
Augustine, 50

baptism, 91, 116, 122
Belgic Confession, 16, 18, 23
believers: conscience of, 40, 83–85,
87, 90, 93, 117, 126–27; contri-
tion of, 84, 86, 106; fellowship
of, 32, 82, 117; holiness of after
conversion, 32–33, 35, 38–39,
94, 98, 100, 117; before election, 33, 35, 65–66; before the
fall, 64–65, 106; in perseverance, 83, 87, 90–91, 112, 127
Beza, Theodore, 16–17
Bible. *See* Scripture
blasphemy, 40, 125
Bogerman, Johannes, 17, 23

calling, of God: efficiency of, 32,
35, 64, 69–74, 94, 107, 109,
120–21; general earnest, 68–70,
98, 124–25; irrevocable, 34–35,

Scripture Index

ALSO AVAILABLE
from
KEVIN DEYOUNG

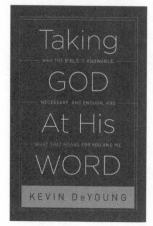

For more information, visit **crossway.org**.